Praise for the First Edition:

"Are you interested in capitalism as a path to your personal utopia? This stirring moral defense of a free society is the place to start."

—*Tyler Cowen, George Mason University, USA*

"In forceful strokes, Jason Brennan attacks the work of the late G. A. Cohen's defense of socialism and neatly shows why and how it is not the best of all systems even in the best of all possible worlds, let alone the highly imperfect world in which we live. His combination of accessible prose with technical precision is a model of good writing on political theory that should enable this book to reach the wider audience it deserves."

—*Richard Epstein, New York University, USA*

"Gone is the false triumphalism of the 1990s. The question of how to organize society, and the ideological conflict between market systems and socialist systems, is live. Brennan offers in this brief volume a fully realized and compelling answer to Jerry Cohen's rightly celebrated book *Why Not Socialism?* Many of the responses to socialist advocacy dismiss command economies as impractical or impossible. But Brennan grants Cohen his premises, and carries out the argument in a way that faithfully mirrors the logic that Cohen tried to marshal in his defense of socialism. Brennan offers an unflinching defense of capitalism, and does it with style and humor. His writing is at once accessible to the first-time philosopher and yet persuasive to the denizens of the ivory towers. This book will be on the reading list for every class I teach."

—*Michael Munger, Duke University, USA*

Why
Not Capitalism?

Most people believe capitalism is a compromise with selfish human nature. As Adam Smith put it, "It is not from the benevolence of the butcher, the brewer, or the baker, that we expect our dinner, but from their regard to their own interest." Capitalism works better than socialism, according to this thinking, only because we are not kind and generous enough to make socialism work. If we were saints, we would be socialists.

In *Why Not Capitalism?*, Jason Brennan attacks this widely held belief, arguing that capitalism would remain the best system even if we were morally perfect. Even then, private property and free markets would be the best way to realize mutual cooperation, social justice, harmony, and prosperity. Socialists seek to capture the moral high ground by showing that ideal socialism is morally superior to realistic capitalism. But, Brennan responds, ideal capitalism is superior to ideal socialism, and so capitalism beats socialism at every level.

Clearly, engagingly, and at times provocatively written, *Why Not Capitalism?* will cause readers of all political persuasions to re-evaluate where they stand vis-à-vis economic priorities and systems—as they exist now and as they might be improved in the future.

In this expanded second edition, Brennan responds to his critics throughout the book and provides two new, final chapters. One argues against egalitarianism in a capitalist utopia because egalitarianism frequently misdiagnoses the problems (for example, the problem with poverty isn't that poor people have *less* but that they don't have *enough*). The other new chapter shows that we don't need to be angels in an anarchic utopia, but merely decent people who are willing to adhere to four undemanding moral principles.

Jason Brennan is the Robert J. and Elizabeth Flanagan Family Professor of Strategy, Economics, Ethics, and Public Policy at the McDonough School of Business, Georgetown University, USA. He is the author of sixteen books, including *Why It's OK to Want to Be Rich* (2020) and *In Defense of Openness* (2018). His books have been translated over thirty times into sixteen languages. He is the editor of *Public Affairs Quarterly*.

JASON BRENNAN

Why Not Capitalism?

Second Edition

Routledge
Taylor & Francis Group
NEW YORK AND LONDON

Second edition published 2024
by Routledge
605 Third Avenue, New York, NY 10158

and by Routledge
4 Park Square, Milton Park, Abingdon, Oxon OX14 4RN

Routledge is an imprint of the Taylor & Francis Group, an informa business

First edition published 2014 by Routledge.

Library of Congress Cataloguing-in-Publication Data
Names: Brennan, Jason, 1979- author.
Title: Why not capitalism? / Jason Brennan.
Description: Second edition. | New York, NY : Routledge, 2024. | Includes bibliographical references and index.
Identifiers: LCCN 2023052077 (print) | LCCN 2023052078 (ebook) | ISBN 9781032730103 (hardback) | ISBN 9781032730127 (paperback) | ISBN 9781003424116 (ebook)
Subjects: LCSH: Capitalism.
Classification: LCC HB501 .B7456 2024 (print) | LCC HB501 (ebook) | DDC 330.12/2--dc23/eng/20231130
LC record available at https://lccn.loc.gov/2023052077
LC ebook record available at https://lccn.loc.gov/2023052078

ISBN: 978-1-032-73010-3 (hbk)
ISBN: 978-1-032-73012-7 (pbk)
ISBN: 978-1-003-42411-6 (ebk)

DOI: 10.4324/9781003424116

Typeset in Joanna and Din
by MPS Limited, Dehradun

Contents

Acknowledgements from the First Edition

My mentor David Schmidtz once said, in conversation, "Don't concede the moral high ground." I've also heard him say that a proper defense of markets has to be in the language of morality, not just the language of economics. This book is written in that spirit.

Thanks to John Tomasi, David Schmidtz, David Estlund, Corey Brettschneider, Sharon Krause, Greg Weinar, Pete Boettke, Loren Lomasky, John Hasnas, Peter Jaworski, Kevin Vallier, Michael Heumer, Bryan Caplan, Thomas Cushman, and James Otteson, with whom I've had many fruitful conversations about these topics over the years. Thanks twice to Tomasi for suggesting I turn the *Mickey Mouse Clubhouse* thought experiment, which I had used simply as a teaching tool, into a short book. Thanks to audiences at the University of Arizona, University of Toronto, University of New Orleans, Bowling Green State University, the American Philosophical Society, Georgetown University's Hoyas for Liberty, and students at Brown University, Georgetown University, and Wellesley College for their valuable feedback and criticism. Thanks to Andy Beck at Routledge for his enthusiasm for the project and for his aid in seeing how the argument could go beyond mere parody.

Finally, thanks to Keaton and Aiden Brennan, ages 2 and 5, for their research support, upon which this book greatly depends.

Jason Brennan
Washington, DC
September 2013

Notes on the Second Edition

The first edition was short and sweet. It said what it needed to say. The challenge now is to ensure the second edition adds what needs to be added without getting too long.

The most common question I received is whether utopian capitalism should be as egalitarian as utopian socialism. Chapter 5 gives my response. I think egalitarianism often misdiagnoses what the problems are and thus offers incorrect solutions. Egalitarianism is often motivated by bad or irrelevant analogies. In particular, Cohen's own original argument for egalitarianism leads to conclusions no one, including him, wants to endorse.

This is a book responding to the idea that people would be socialist if only they were angels—if only they were fully good. I argue, on the contrary, that capitalism is best even for angels. However, Chapter 6 argues that the demands of utopian anarchist capitalism turn out not to be all that demanding. It doesn't require angelic behavior; it requires that we're all minimally decent. We fall short not because aren't angels, but because many of us are downright bad.

This second edition incorporates some generally reworded and abridged excerpts from previously published work, including work responding to responses to the first edition:

Jason Brennan, "Community and Diversity in G. A. Cohen's Socialist Ideal," *Analyse & Kritik* 37 (2015): 113–130.

Jason Brennan, "*Private Governance* and the Three Biases of Political Philosophy," *Review of Austrian Economics* 31 (2018): 235–243.

Jason Brennan, "'Get a Job and Pay Your Taxes!': What Utopophiles Must Say to the Western Poor," *Social Philosophy and Policy* 39 (2022): 48–67.

Jason Brennan and Christopher Freiman, "Why Not Anarchism?," *Politics, Philosophy, and Economics* 21 (2022): 415–436.

Few observers are inclined to find fault with capitalism as an engine of production. Criticism usually proceeds either from moral or cultural disapproval of certain features of the capitalist system, or from the short-run vicissitudes (crises and depressions) with which long-run improvement is interspersed.

—1964 *Encyclopaedia Britannica* entry on *capitalism*

Deep Down, Everyone's a Socialist ... and Wrong

One

CAPITALISM: NASTY THEORY, RIGHT SPECIES?

Michael Moore ends his film *Capitalism: A Love Story* with a catechism: "Capitalism is an evil, and you cannot regulate evil. You have to eliminate it and replace it with something that is good for all people, and that something is democracy." By "democracy," Moore means collective control of the means of production—that is, socialism. Yet, even after spending 127 minutes exposing the evils of capitalism, Moore won't just come out and say that we need to replace capitalism with socialism. Why not?

The term "socialism" appeared, but was buried deep within, the Occupy Wall Street website, despite its repeated invections against the economic status quo and its vague call for "a new socio-political and economic alternative."

Moore and the Occupy Wall Street organizers know that many Americans think "socialism" is a dirty word with a dirty history. Many accept a common historical account: In the twentieth century, the world experimented with two great social systems. The countries that tried different forms of capitalism—for instance, the United States, Denmark, Switzerland, Australia, Japan, Singapore, Hong Kong, and South Korea—all became rich. Consider: the US considers the poverty line for an American living alone to be about $13,500.

DOI: 10.4324/9781003424116-1

A person living in the United States off this meager income, adjusting for the cost of living, is still among the richest 20% of people alive today, earning multiple times the income of the typical person worldwide.[1] In contrast, the countries that tried socialism—the Soviet Union, China, Cuba, Vietnam, Cambodia, and North Korea—were hellholes. Socialist governments murdered around 100 million (and perhaps many more) of their own citizens, making socialism about as lethal as the fourteenth-century black plague.[2] In socialist countries no one got rich, except maybe a few Communist Party officials. Socialism was especially bad for poor proletariat workers, the very people the system was supposed to help the most. So, sure, capitalism has problems, as Michael Moore and Occupy Wall Street can show you, with perhaps some exaggeration here and there. But socialism was a disaster. In short: we had a live-action debate between capitalism and socialism, and capitalism won.

Despite this, many people who oppose socialism and support markets find capitalism morally uninspiring. Sure, capitalism performs better than socialism. But, we worry, that is just because people are so selfish.

Capitalism rewards us for developing greater talent or working in critical jobs. It pays us for innovation and efficiency. In general, the more you do for others on the market, the better you get paid. We respond to those incentives, and so it works. Socialism asks us to work hard for the sake of others, without wanting more for ourselves than what others get. We refuse to play along, so it doesn't work. But many people worry this shows we are not altruistic or fraternal enough for socialism.

In the twentieth century, we learned that the great power wielded by socialist governments attracts sociopaths and tyrants. Yet, again, we worry that this is just because we are so morally flawed. Socialism asks us to supply benevolent philosopher-kings, but the best we produce is a Pol Pot, Stalin, or Mao. It seems the problem is with us.

Since we are selfish, greedy, and fearful, maybe market-based economies are the best we can do. If only men were angels, though, we could dispense with capitalism and make socialism work. Utopia is socialist. Or so many people think.

Even capitalism's greatest defenders seem to agree. Adam Smith tells us, "It is not from the benevolence of the butcher, the brewer, or the baker, that we expect our dinner, but from their regard to their own interest. We address ourselves, not to their humanity but to their self-love ..."[3] Bernard Mandeville, in his famous poem "The Grumbling Hive," says capitalism runs on vice much like biodiesel engines run on food waste. He asks us to imagine a hive full of selfish bees, each trying to make a buck by supplying others' "lust and vanity." Yet while, "every Part" of this capitalist system is "full of Vice," the "whole Mass [is] a Paradise."[4] Even "the very Poor Lived better than the Rich before."[5] Later in the poem, Mandeville imagines that the bees become virtuous, unselfish, and motivated to pursue spiritual endeavors. But then, without greed, the economy falls apart. Finally, there's Ayn Rand, "Goddess of the Market,"[6] who defends capitalism by arguing that selfishness is a virtue and altruism is evil.[7]

Socialism seems to answer to a higher moral calling. Perhaps the best evidence of this is that socialists today defend their view in *moral* terms, while capitalists defend their view in *economic* terms.[8] The defenders of capitalism focus on capitalism's results. The defenders of socialism focus on their own good intentions. Socialists ask us to imagine how good the world could be, if only we were better.

The problem with socialism thus seems to be that it demands too much of us—it asks us to love our neighbors as ourselves, to share, and to never take advantage of power. Socialism seems like a noble idea—and we're not *good enough* for it. Socialism says, "All for one and one for all." But we're more comfortable with, "Every man for himself." And so, sociobiologist Edward Wilson jokes of socialism: "Wonderful theory, wrong species."[9]

SO, WHY NOT SOCIALISM?

You, the reader, are probably not a socialist. (Most people who call themselves socialist aren't really; they instead defend a form of capitalism with regulatory welfare states.) But you probably accept the view just described, the view that markets are a kind of moral compromise, the view that if we could harness the best within us, we would dispense with capitalism. If you are a typical person, you probably agree that socialism would be best if only human beings were much nicer than they in fact are.

The best spokesperson of this widely shared view is the philosopher G. A. ("Jerry") Cohen. Cohen was the leading Marxist philosopher—and one of the leading political philosophers, period—of the past century. Capitalism has had countless critics, but Cohen is perhaps its best *moral* critic. *Why Not Capitalism?* is in a way a debate with Cohen. I want to show he, and everyone else who agrees with him, is mistaken. I debate Cohen in order to undermine the widespread belief that socialism is morally superior to capitalism. To defend capitalism means overcoming objections like his.

Shortly after his death in 2009, Cohen published a short book called *Why Not Socialism?* It argues that only socialism can be just. Capitalism, Cohen claims, is an inherently repugnant way for us to live together.

Though *Why Not Socialism?* is tiny—82 pages, about 10,000 words—it "punches well above its weight," as a reviewer in the *Guardian* says.[10] Philosopher Jonathan Wolff finds the book's argument "disarming." Ellen Meiksins Wood thinks Cohen "says things that need to be said ..."[11] Alexander Barker says that we, the readers, "are challenged and ultimately persuaded that our objections to socialism are practical rather than moral. We in turn must confront the question of how to lead our lives according to these ideals in our less-than-ideal world."[12] Andrew Stone agrees that the book is "stimulating and thoughtfully argued advocacy of the better world that we need to fight for."[13]

Cohen's book contains a simple but powerful thought experiment meant to prove that socialism really is inherently *morally superior* to capitalism, even if capitalism "works better." Cohen means to prove our worries about capitalism are correct. For Cohen, to say of socialism, "Wonderful theory, wrong species" is to damn humanity, not socialism. Capitalism works better only because it harnesses our greed and fear. But socialism is the system of love and community. Socialism is not bad for us; the problem is that we are bad for socialism.

THE CAMPING TRIP ARGUMENT FOR SOCIALISM

Cohen has a simple argument for the inherent moral superiority of socialism. Unlike many Marxists, he doesn't rely on convoluted dialectics, falsified and confused economic theories, or postmodernist piffle. Unlike many history professors, he doesn't try to discredit capitalist economists by lying about their views or engaging in quote alteration and fabrication.

Rather, he just wants you to imagine a camping trip. Once you reflect on how you'd like to run a camping trip, he thinks you'll see that, regardless of whether you call yourself a libertarian, capitalist, left-liberal, moderate, conservative, integralist, communitarian, social democrat, or whatnot, you probably already believe deep down that socialism would be best.

In this section, I summarize Cohen's entire argument in *Why Not Socialism?*. I'll also add in additional supporting arguments to help him make his case. I intend to knock Cohen's entire argument down, but not before I help him build it up as much as I can.

Cohen first has us imagine a camping trip among friends. Everyone wants everyone to have a great time. When the campers bring their equipment to the campsite, they stop asserting ownership rights over their stuff, and instead treat everything as a common bounty. Food and goods are held in common and shared freely. Everyone works hard to ensure everyone has what she needs. They take turns doing the hard work. The campers maintain a perfect community of perfect equality.

That's how a camping trip among friends should go. But, Cohen says, notice that the campers are living by socialist principles. They make sure everyone is equal in status, does equal work, and enjoys an equal quality of life. They share everything as a collective. Everyone does her part. On an ideal camping trip like this, people act like socialists.

Now, Cohen says, imagine what the camping trip would look like if the campers began to act like people do in real-life capitalism. Imagine Harry demands better food because he is good at fishing. He refuses to put his skills to use unless he gets the best fish. Sylvia demands privileges after she finds an apple tree in the woods. She refuses to share unless she gets a break from the communal chores. Leslie demands extra payment for her special knowledge of how to crack nuts. Morgan, whose father left him a well-stocked pond 30 years ago, gloats over having more food than the others.

Cohen asks, isn't "the socialist way, with collective property and planned mutual giving, rather obviously the *best* way to run a camping trip …?"[14] Cohen claims the camping trip was clearly better when the campers acted like socialists. When the campers started acting like capitalists, the trip became stifling and repulsive.

It is hard to disagree. When Harry says he'll catch more fish only if he gets the choicest catch, he comes across as a schmuck.[15] Friends don't talk that way to each other. Morgan brags at his good fortune: "Great. Now I can have better food than you guys have."[16] What a jerk! But, Cohen says, these repugnant behaviors are just what we see in real-life capitalist societies.[17]

Cohen then articulates the moral principles that underlie the socialist version of the camping trip. These moral principles explain how the socialist campers relate to one another, and why their camping trip seems morally superior to modern capitalist societies.

First, the principle of *socialist equality of opportunity* eliminates all inequalities resulting from undeserved disadvantages or advantages. So, for instance, the principle forbids people from having more simply because they happen to inherit greater natural talents or were born to rich parents. After all, no one did anything to deserve being born with such good fortune. This principle allows significant inequalities only if these inequalities result from people's choices. The principle explains why Morgan shouldn't have more fish: he's just lucky that his grandfather left him a well-stocked pond.

Second, the campers also abide by a *socialist principle of community*. The campers care about one another, and care that they care about one another. Cohen argues that as a result, the campers will not tolerate the inequalities that socialist equality of opportunity would otherwise permit. So, while socialist equality of opportunity allows only those inequalities that result from free choice, the socialist principle of community forbids any inequalities that would put distance among the campers. Cohen claims that we cannot be fully in community with one another if we are unequal. After all, if I am rich and you are poor, then I just can't fully understand your problems. Inequality prevents us from empathizing with each other.[18] (To see why, imagining complaining to Bill Gates about being late on your mortgage. Could Gates really empathize with you, and wouldn't you find it a bit absurd to discuss financial difficulties with a billionaire?) When one person is much richer or poorer than the others, it cuts that person off from communal life, or so Cohen claims.[19] This principle explains why the campers will choose to work toward perfect equality, rather than allowing some to become worse off as a result of poor choices.

You might not accept Cohen's favored principles of justice. He doesn't much argue for them in this short book. But Cohen would say he needn't rely on them too much for his argument. For him, what's important is that you agree that the camping trip is better when it was socialist and egalitarian than when it became capitalist and inegalitarian.

The socialist camping trip is just a trip among friends. It's not really a society—it's more of a short-term microsociety. Still, Cohen asks, wouldn't life just obviously be better if we could somehow make large-scale societies more like the camping trip?

Put aside for now the question of whether we *can* do so. There are lots of things we can't do or might not be able to do that we know are good to do. It might be impossible to prevent the next pandemic, but it would be better if we could. It might be impossible to discover many important scientific truths, but it would be better if we could. It might be impossible to develop efficient, pollution-free energy, but it would be better if we could. Judgments about what's intrinsically good are independent of judgments of what's feasible.

So, imagine we had a magic wand that would make the entire world just like the socialist camping trip. Obviously, we have no such wand. But Cohen's question is, if we had such a wand, should we wave it? Cohen says, of course! If we could somehow discover how to make societies run like the socialist camping trip, we would rejoice.

If so, this means we tolerate capitalism only because we think we must. We tolerate capitalism only because we don't know how to make socialism work as intended. Perhaps, given our moral and cognitive failings, capitalism "delivers the goods."[20] But socialism would be the preferred system if only human beings were morally better, like the people on the socialist version of camping trip. On Cohen's view, human vice is in abundance. Capitalism works because it channels that vice toward publicly beneficial ends. Capitalism works only because it relies upon greed, fear, and people's limited knowledge. But socialism, he says, would rely upon generosity, community, and wisdom, all in short supply.

Cohen says there are two distinct questions about socialism. First, is it intrinsically *desirable?* The camping trip thought experiment proves it is. Second, is it *feasible?* Here he is less certain. He thinks it might be feasible, but is unsure.

Many people believe socialism is infeasible. Cohen responds that whether something is feasible has no bearing on whether it is *intrinsically* desirable. Whether it is possible to get something has no bearing on whether the thing is, in itself, worth having. We can see that just by asking, if it were feasible, would we want it? If it were possible to get it, would we want it? And Cohen thinks he has already shown that we'd all say yes to socialism.

In his previous work, Cohen illustrates this point with an analogy. Suppose you find some grapes. Suppose, somehow, you know these are the tastiest grapes in the world. That is, if you were to eat them, you would find them better tasting than any other grapes. However, suppose the grapes are out of reach. That does not make the grapes any less intrinsically desirable.[21] The fact that you cannot reach the best grapes does not make the grapes less tasty. They are still the best grapes! It just means that the best grapes you can reach are not the best grapes there are.

On Cohen's behalf, I'll defend his point further by borrowing (and modifying) a similar example from the philosopher David Estlund.[22] Suppose we go out for a picnic. On a hill in the distance, we see the perfect picnic spot. We can tell from here that this picnic spot is better than any other. It's much better than our current spot. However, suppose it is difficult, impossible, or just too costly to get there. Suppose, for instance, that to get to the spot, we would have to cross a deep ravine, a briar patch, and a swamp filled with alligators. Suppose there's also magical fog surrounding the hill. This fog transforms morally imperfect people like you and me into murderous monsters like Pol Pot and Mao, but it has no effect on perfectly virtuous people.[23] Faced with such obstacles, we should not bother to try to reach the perfect picnic spot. Yet, none of these obstacles make the picnic spot on the hill any less perfect or desirable in itself. The picnic spot, in itself, is still better than any spot we will reach. If we *could* get to that better spot, without having to suffer the costs of doing so, then we should. We shouldn't bother try to get to this perfect spot, but the problem is the barriers around the spot, not the spot itself.

Here is a different analogy to sell Cohen's point. Suppose you are the market for a sports car. You can choose between the 2013 Chevrolet Camaro ZL1 or the 2012 BMW M6. The experts at *Car and Driver* say, "The BMW is the better car by nearly every measure."[24] They claim it is the better car, period. Yet, they also recommend you buy the ZL1 instead of the M6. They conclude, "The BMW does most everything better. But the ZL1 has more than half the swagger at just less than half the price."[25] In short, the Camaro is the better car *for the price*, but the BMW is the intrinsically better car. The BMW is still intrinsically more desirable. If you could have either car *for free*, you should pick the M6.

And that's much like Cohen's point. If we could get socialism to work and we could transition to socialism at a low enough cost, of course we'd want to. So, he concludes, socialism is inherently morally superior to capitalism.

Now turn to the question of whether socialism is feasible. Many economists are convinced pure socialism cannot work. Even Cohen agrees, partly. Here, I'll explain why.

Every economic system needs three things to function.[26] First, the system needs information—it needs some way to coordinate people's actions, to convey to people what they need to do in light of what others are doing. Second, it needs incentives—it needs some way to induce people to act on the information they receive. Third, because people make mistakes, it needs learning—a process by which people become better at responding to incentives and information.

When economists claim socialism is infeasible or unworkable, they cite two different kinds of reasons. First—the most familiar—is an *incentive* problem. Socialism might be infeasible because of human beings' *moral* limitations. Socialist governments have great power. Murderous, power-hungry sociopaths try to seize control of that power. Socialism also fails to motivate selfish people to work hard for the sake of others. In practice, "from each according to his ability, to each according to his needs" fails to meet needs or get people to make use of their abilities. But if people were virtuous, they would not be corrupted or tempted by power. They would work hard for the common good without demanding extra rewards. Economists, of course, don't use moral language like this. They just say that most people are insufficiently altruistic to make socialist institutions function.

Second, socialism might be infeasible because of an *information* problem. This second problem with socialism may be unfamiliar to you unless you have a strong background in economics. Economists say socialism fails because socialist economic planners lack the information they need to make it work. Socialism fails because of our *cognitive* limitations.

In economic theory, the "Socialist Calculation Problem" or "Knowledge Problem" holds that in large-scale societies, it is impossible to make good economic calculations without market prices or a good substitute for market prices. Market prices are not arbitrary numbers set by capricious managers.[27] They are a function of supply and demand. Market prices emerge from the decisions made by all actors in market, based on their own needs, values, and knowledge of the ever-changing conditions around them. Market prices thus convey information about the relative scarcity of goods in light of the effective demand for those goods. Market prices thus tell producers and consumers how to adjust their behavior to other people's wants and needs.

So, for instance, if more industries start buying aluminum, the sellers of aluminum will try to raise their prices. When Coca-Cola notices that the price of aluminum is rising, it will look for ways to use less aluminum. In fact, soda cans use much less aluminum now than they did 40 years ago, but the cans have a better design that allows them to be stacked high despite containing less metal. This is not because Coca-Cola executives are environmentalists, but because they benefit from cutting costs.

Or, suppose there's a power outage. You rush to the store for ice to keep your beer cold. But when you get to the store, you find the now scarce ice is selling for $12 a bag.[28] You'll probably decide it's not worth buying ice for your beer. What you don't realize, though, is that by choosing not to buy the ice, you thereby leave it for the diabetic who needs it to cool his insulin. As economics textbooks say, market prices tend to ensure goods go to their highest value uses. (Remember: tend, not guarantee.)

Consider a simple object—a number 2 pencil. You might not realize it, but literally millions of people worked together to produce that pencil, though only a few hundred of them knew they were doing so. The person who mines the iron that will go into the ball bearings in machines that help make the ink that will end up on the pencil might have little idea that he is helping to make pencils. Yet market prices bring these millions of people together to produce pencils.

Few people, aside from academic economists, understand what market prices are, how prices convey information, and how such prices coordinate billions of people to work together. But the magic of prices is that they help us work together even though most people don't understand what prices mean. People don't need to understand how the market works for the market to work. Prices motivate people to act on the information contained inside the price without requiring people to understand that prices contain information.

Socialism dispenses with the market economy and thus with market prices. But no one can run an economy without information. Socialism thus needs some substitute for market prices. According to the Calculation Problem, large-scale socialist planning cannot work, even if everyone were motivated to make it work, because planners do not have a substitute for prices. The problem of planning an economy is too hard.[29] The problem isn't people's *morals*; even if we were all morally perfect, the Calculation Problem would remain.

Unlike many Marxists, Cohen concedes that "bourgeois economics" is basically sound.[30] Marxists used to argue that socialism would be more efficient and productive than capitalism. Cohen concedes that capitalism won this battle. Cohen even concedes that large-scale economies need some sort of market with market prices to work.

Cohen is more impressed with Marx's *moral* critique of capitalism than his *economic* critique.[31] Cohen appreciates that the Calculation Problem casts strong doubts on the feasibility of socialism.[32] However, Cohen says, even if large-scale pure socialism is not feasible, perhaps "market socialism"—a kind of hybrid of capitalism and socialism—is feasible. At the very least, Cohen claims, we do not *know* market socialism is infeasible.

Cohen thus ends his defense of socialism by citing the work of political scientist Joseph Carens, who claims market socialism can combine socialist distributive principles with the market's information-gathering power.[33] In Carens's scheme, the means of production are publicly owned, but managers compete with each other on the market. Their profits are shared with everyone. Cohen acknowledges that few economists find Carens's arguments convincing, and Cohen does not try to solve the problems critics see in Carens's work.

In summary: The socialist camping trip was wonderful, but the capitalist camping trip was awful. It would clearly be better if we could, somehow, make the whole world like the socialist camping trip. This shows that socialism is inherently morally superior to capitalism, regardless of whether this kind of socialism is feasible. Even if pure socialism on a large scale is not feasible, there may at least be a type of socialism that is. Finally, Cohen asks us not to lose hope. He concludes, "every market … is a system of predation. Our attempt to get beyond predation has thus far failed. I do not think the right conclusion is to give up."[34]

THE FORCE OF THE ARGUMENT

Cohen seems to have a simple, powerful proof of the following claims:

1. Socialism is intrinsically more desirable than capitalism. If we could make socialism work, we'd want to.
2. If we are stuck with capitalism, it's because we are too hardhearted or dumb to do better.

3. Capitalism only works because it runs on—indeed, exacerbates—selfishness, fear, and greed.

In short, we are right to be suspicious of capitalism. Cohen thinks he has shown us that deep down, we all share his moral revulsion of the market.

That doesn't mean you'd vote the same way Cohen would. You and he might disagree about how close we can get to a functional form of socialism. You might be more pessimistic about the prospects for real-world socialism than Cohen. You might be more or less pessimistic about how well the regulatory welfare state or social democracy works.

I teach Cohen's book in introductory political economy and political philosophy courses at least once a year. Few of my students call themselves socialists. Most of them favor some form of welfare-state capitalism over socialism.

Most of them just say, "Well, sure, I suppose it would be better if we all lived like the people on the camping trip, but real people just aren't like that." Cohen's response, I tell them, would be that perhaps people could be like that, if capitalism hadn't amplified their selfish tendencies. But, even if people are naturally too selfish for socialism, all Cohen wants is for the students to agree that it would be better if we all lived like the people on the camping trip. "People aren't like that" is, in Cohen's words, a *factual*, not a *normative* defense of inequality.[35] (A factual claim describes how things are; a normative claim describes how things *ought* or *ought not* to be.) As Cohen summarizes it:

> A prominent factual defense of inequality traces it to a supposedly ineradicable human selfishness. This defense says that inequality is ensured by something as original to human

> nature as sin is, on the Christian view of original sin: people are by nature selfish, whether or not that is, like being a sinner, a bad thing to be, and inequality is an unavoidable result of that selfishness, whether or not that inequality is just.[36]

Cohen is right: This is not a moral justification of inequality. It is merely an empirical assertion that inequality is inevitable.

Or, some students say, "You can't judge human nature. Human nature isn't good or bad; it just is." Cohen would respond, "If you had a magic wand that would make people less greedy, rapacious, and nasty, and more kind, loving, and generous, you'd wave that magic wand. And that shows that you actually are judging human nature."

Or, some students say, "But I wouldn't be willing to work that hard for everybody else if I didn't get paid more." Here I remind them that Cohen isn't advocating that they work hard while others live in idleness off their efforts. Cohen doesn't think talented should become slaves to the lazy or untalented. In Cohen's ideal society, everyone works equally hard and everyone gets an equal reward. But, still, some students balk and say they wouldn't feel motivated under this scheme. Cohen's response is that this is because they are selfish and unjust. Cohen doesn't claim moral superiority, though. He'd admit that he's similarly selfish and unjust.

Or, other students said that they don't think that they should be *forced* to treat everyone else in the world as their friend. But, I remind them, Cohen is not here advocating that we *force* you to work for others as if everyone in the world is your friend. Instead, Cohen is saying that if we were all good and just, we would thereby *want* to treat everyone else as friends. In a perfectly just world, a world full of people who always choose to do what's right, Cohen's socialism would be voluntary. Cohen's ideal form of socialism is not the USSR, but voluntary anarchist socialism which doesn't require a coercive government at all.

To my surprise, most of my pro-market philosopher and economist colleagues often have no stronger objections to Cohen than my students. They might say that Cohen is arguing that the whole world should be like the family, and then say that of course we don't have that strong a capacity for love.[37] Or, they may recite some institutional economics, or argue that justice is about dealing with our flaws, not imagining them away. Many of them just dismiss Cohen as too utopian.

But these are no objections! This is vigorous agreement disguised as vigorous disagreement.

Saying Cohen is too utopian concedes the moral high ground to Cohen and concedes his main conclusion. It concedes that capitalism works well only because it is, as Cohen says, a "social technology"[38] that uses "base motives to productive economic effect."[39] It concedes that the market "recruits low-grade motives to desirable ends."[40] It does not answer Cohen's charge that the "market is intrinsically repugnant."[41] To dismiss socialism as too utopian is to say that it's *best*, but unattainable.

Cohen's argument requires a different kind of response.

In my view, Cohen's argument fails, and fails badly, in a way that's suddenly obvious once you point it out. In Chapter 2—"The Mickey Mouse Clubhouse Argument for Capitalism"—I will perform some philosophical aikido. I will parody Cohen's style of argument to show, on the contrary, that capitalism is more intrinsically desirable than socialism. I will show how Cohen's kind of argument for socialism turns into an even better argument for capitalism.

Chapter 2 parodies Cohen by imitating the same structure, format, and tone of his argument. However, while Cohen describes an idealized socialist camping trip, I describe an idealized capitalist society, as presented in the children's show *The Mickey Mouse Clubhouse*, a CGI-animated cartoon on the Disney, Jr. channel. In effect, I copy Cohen's argument, but flip his argument around to get the opposite result.

Part of my goal is to expose—through parody—that Cohen's argument for socialism is fallacious. When you see how easily his argument for socialism can be flipped to produce an even better argument for capitalism, you'll see that Cohen's argument is flawed. I'll explain what the flaw is in Chapter 3, but there's a good chance you'll see it before I explain it.

However, I do not just mean this to be a mere parody or *reductio ad absurdum* of Cohen. I am not simply trying to say that Cohen's argument for socialism fails and leave it at that.

Instead, I intend this exercise to vindicate the intrinsic moral goodness of capitalism. Contrary to Cohen, we are not stuck with capitalism because people are too selfish, greedy, and fearful to make socialism work. Rather, even if people had morally perfect motivations, we would still have grounds to prefer capitalism. Capitalism is not merely better economics than socialism for the real world. Even in utopia, capitalism occupies the *moral* high ground. Capitalism with bad people is better than socialism with bad people. Capitalism with mediocre people is better than socialism with mediocre people. Capitalism with good people is better than socialism with good people. Capitalism with flawless people is better than socialism with flawless people.

I'll concede that the title of this book, *Why Not Capitalism?*, may seem at first glance a bit odd to any Western reader.

After all, we *have* various forms capitalism in abundance, perhaps more so now than at any other time in the world's history, though we have few fully free-market capitalist economies. But my hope is that its double meaning may be apparent now, at the conclusion of this first chapter. The title of course signals that the book is a direct rejoinder to Cohen's popular book, *Why Not Socialism?* But I also chose it to ask the question it poses more generally, and as a moral rather than merely an economic query. So, in the chapters that follow, I attempt to answer the question in *moral* terms, arguing that the best possible society is a capitalistic society.

The Mickey Mouse Clubhouse Argument for Capitalism: A Parody

Two

A NOTE TO READERS

This chapter is a parody of G. A. Cohen's *Why Not Socialism?* I will closely follow Cohen's writing style, diction, tone, phrasing, format, and argumentative structure. Much of the time, I will be paraphrasing or quoting Cohen directly.

I will write with about the same level of philosophical rigor and depth as he did. Cohen's book isn't a treatise; neither is this chapter. Cohen doesn't consider and defeat all possible objections; neither do I.

Cohen uses a thought experiment about an imaginary camping trip to argue that socialism is better than capitalism. I will follow Cohen's style of argument, but instead substitute the imaginary village from the TV show *Mickey Mouse Clubhouse* to argue that capitalism is better than socialism. Note that I am not talking about *The Mickey Mouse Club*—the old black-and-white show from the 1950s—but the more recent CGI cartoon available on various Disney channels.

If you are a socialist, you might find the argument in this chapter stupid or nonsensical. Hang tight. We'll discuss what's going on in Chapters 3 or 4.

Remember that my goal here is not simply to expose, via parody, that Cohen's argument for socialism is defective. Even though Cohen's argument is fallacious, he is on to

DOI: 10.4324/9781003424116-2

something. Cohen's ultimate legacy—the ultimate result of his life's work defending socialism—will be to help us see that from a moral point of view, the intrinsically best society is capitalist. Cohen also became famous in part for criticizing the libertarian philosopher Robert Nozick.[1] In Chapter 4, I'll explain that another legacy of Cohen's work will be to show that Nozick was basically right all along about the nature of utopia.

WHY NOT CAPITALISM?

The question that forms the title of this book is not intended rhetorically. I begin by presenting what I believe to be a compelling *preliminary* case for capitalism. I then ask why that case might be thought to be *merely* preliminary, why, that is, it might, in the end, be defeated: I try to see how well the preliminary case stacks up on further reflection.

To summarize more specifically: In section I, I describe a context, called "the Mickey Mouse Clubhouse Village," in which most people would, I think, strongly favor a capitalist form of life over feasible alternatives. Section II specifies five principles—voluntary community, respect, reciprocity, social justice, and beneficence—that are realized in the Mickey Mouse Clubhouse Village, and whose realization explains, so I believe, why the Mickey Mouse Clubhouse Village mode of organization is attractive. In section III, I ask whether those principles also make (society-wide) capitalism *desirable*. But I also ask, in section IV, whether capitalism is *feasible*, by discussing difficulties that face the project of promoting capitalism's principles not in the mere small, within the confined space of the Mickey Mouse Clubhouse Village, but throughout the world as a whole, in a permanent way. Section V is a short coda.

I

THE MICKEY MOUSE CLUBHOUSE VILLAGE

Mickey Mouse, Minnie Mouse, Donald Duck, Daisy Duck, Goofy, Clarabelle Cow, and Professor Ludwig von Drake, and many other characters, live together in a village. There is no hierarchy among them.[2] They have separate goals and projects, but also share common aims, such as the goal that each of them should have a fulfilling life and good time, doing, so far as possible, the kind of projects that they like best or find most meaningful. Some of these projects they do together; some they do separately.

They have various facilities to carry out their different projects. For example, there are communal spaces, such as amphitheaters, racetracks, obstacles courses, and parks. They avail themselves of these facilities collectively. They have shared understandings of who is going to use what and when, under what circumstances, and why.

There are also privately owned spaces and things. Mickey Mouse owns a clubhouse that he shares with his friends. Minnie owns and runs a "Bowtique": a hair bow factory and store. She employs Daisy Duck, paying her a fair wage and treating her as an end in herself. Clarabelle Cow owns and runs a "Moo Mart" sundries store and a "Moo Muffin" factory. Donald Duck and Willie the Giant own farms. Professor von Drake owns various inventions, including a time machine and a nanotech machine that can manufacture "mouseketools" on command.

There are differences among the villagers, but their mutual understandings, and their spirit of goodwill, ensure that there are no circumstances to which anyone could mount a principled objection.

In the village, everyone does his or her part. Everyone works hard to add to the social surplus. Everyone trades value for value. Everyone is also free to pursue his or her vision of the good life without having to ask permission from others.

At the same time, all the villagers are extremely kind. If anyone has any unmet needs, the others line up to help her. There is no violence or any threats of violence—force is unnecessary to maintain social order.

Village life is not all about work! The villagers spend much of their time having fun. They enjoy lightly competitive or non-competitive games, going on adventures, and producing art and music. Sometimes they do these activities alone, sometimes together in small groups, and sometimes with everyone as a whole.

When bad luck strikes—e.g., when some baby ducks must be taught to fly, or when a baby dragon is lost, or when the Tick Tock Time Machine accidentally turns half the villagers into babies, or when a Gooey Goo spill creates five copies of Goofy—the villagers happily come together as a team to solve the problem, making use of their different skills and abilities.

The Mickey Mouse Clubhouse villagers cooperate with a common desire that everyone have the freedom and resources to flourish under their own conceptions of the good life. Everyone operates on principles of mutual concern, tolerance, and respect. They live together happily, without envy, glad to trade value for value, glad to give and share, glad to help those in need, and never disposed to free ride, take advantage of, coerce, or subjugate one another.

You could imagine instead a version of the Mickey Mouse Clubhouse Village in which—*as in socialism*—the collective (or its representative, the socialist government) asserts its rights over all pieces of land or equipment, or over everyone's bodies, minds, and talents.[3] You could imagine that the collective or the socialist government decides who will be allowed, for example, to use the hot air balloons, or what color bows Minnie will make, or who will do what work and when, or whether one person's organs should be extracted and given to another.[4] You could base the Mickey Mouse Club Village on the principles of socialist work and strictly collective ownership of everything.

Now, most people would hate that. We probably wouldn't let our children watch that kind of show. Most people would be more drawn to the first kind of Clubhouse Village than to the second, primarily on grounds of fellowship, but also, be it noted, on grounds of efficiency. (I have in mind the inordinate difficulty of trying to have a small board of central planners or even an entire democratic society determine what needs to be done and how to do it.) And this means that most people are drawn to the capitalist ideal, at least in certain restricted settings.

To reinforce this point, consider what it would be like if the villagers stop acting like capitalists and start acting like socialists:

a. Donald decides to forcibly nationalize and control all of the farmland, murdering millions in the process, and causing a massive famine that murders tens of millions more. He uses terror tactics to assert his control. He parrots Lenin: "We shall return to terrorism, and it will be an economic terrorism."[5] But his fellow villagers mutter, in fear, under their breath (when they are sure no one is spying on them), "Oh, for heaven's sake, Donald Duck, don't be such a schmuck. You don't know what these farmlands mean to us, and what role they play in our lives.

You don't know how to farm, what to grow, or how to grow it. Please stop seeing us landowning peasant farmers as enemies of the state!"

b. Things do not go as well as Donald planned, and the other villagers begin to resist. Goofy stifles dissent by creating gulags in the coldest reaches of Disney World. Anyone he deems an enemy is sent to the gulag to be tortured and worked to death. Prisoners receive rations so meager that none have enough energy to meet their work quotas. Yet, the rule of the gulag is that the less they work, the less they eat. And so, the prisoners' bodies wither from starvation and strain, their fingers turn black from frostbite, and their bones break from scurvy. One of Goofy's prisoners thinks, on his second day in the gulag, "Is this unbearable, or is this something I can survive? ... What is it like to break down?"[6] Many prisoners choose to chop off their own feet—they decide they prefer to die of disease in the gulag hospitals than work themselves to death in fields or mines. Many become what other prisoners call the "the goners" or "the garbage-eaters"—inmates insane from hunger and stress, who wander the prison eating shit, dirt, and trash. Only one group flourishes in Goofy's gulag: the *urkas* criminal gang, whom the "gulag officially designate[s]" as "Socially Friendly Elements," whose members "tattoo themselves with masturbating monkeys, who [have] their women assist them in the rapes of nuns and politicals."[7]

c. Mickey Mouse stifles free speech, crushes all political opposition, and installs himself for life as the Premier. He becomes increasingly paranoid. At one point, to assert his control, he murders nearly all members of the governing party. He decides that anyone (aside from himself and his confidantes, such as Professor von Drake) with an education is an enemy of the state, and has them all murdered. He becomes insane with vanity. For instance, when he gives speeches, he has the first audience member to stop applauding killed. He publishes a book *A Short Course on the History of the Revolution in Disney World*. The book is widely read—people treat it as a manual for how to avoid being arrested.[8] Mickey Mouse says, "We stand for organized terror—this is to be frankly admitted … Our aim is to fight against the enemies of the … Government … We judge quickly. In most cases only a day passes between the apprehension of the criminal and his sentence. When confronted with evidence the criminal in almost every case confesses …"[9] Clarabelle Cow assists Mickey by forming a secret police force that spies on all the other villagers. Soon villagers begin to fabricate lies about their neighbors. They claim their neighbors are counterrevolutionaries trying to sabotage the revolution. They know that by turning in their neighbors, they buy themselves a little trust and time. Professor von Drake helps produce massive propaganda to keep the other villagers in line. He cuts off information from the outside world. He begins to lie about science, claiming that socialist physics and biology are different from bourgeois physics and biology.

d. Minnie Mouse creates five-year economic plans for the entire village economy. In some areas, she decides to depopulate the cities and move everyone into agricultural communes. Others she forces to work in factories. She causes massive economic stagnation, shortages, and breadlines. She later visits the capitalist economy of Loony Toons, where Bugs Bunny shows her a model of a six-room Loony Toonsian house, the kind of house that typical steelworkers in Loony Toons were buying. She scoffs, "This is no more representative of typical Loony Toonsian living standards than the Taj Majal was of life in India."[10] Reporters are astonished—Minnie Mouse is a leader, not a pawn, and yet she has no idea how productive capitalism can be.

So, would you rather live in the capitalist or the socialist version of the Mickey Mouse Clubhouse Village? Of course, not everyone would want to live with cartoon mice, ducks, dogs, and cows. But the question I'm asking is not whether you would literally want to live with Mickey Mouse and Donald Duck. Instead, I'm asking wasn't the capitalist way, the way of mutual respect and kindness, with both private and collective property, rather obviously the *best* way to run a village, whether or not you actually *like* Mickey Mouse? Isn't it just obvious that the capitalist version of the village—the actual way the village appears on the show—is far superior to the socialist version?

The circumstances of the Clubhouse Village are multiply special: many features distinguish it from the circumstances of life in a modern society. One may therefore not infer, from the fact that a village of the sort I have described is feasible and desirable, that society-wide capitalism is equally feasible and desirable. There are too many major differences between the contexts for that inference to carry any conviction. What we urgently need to know is precisely *what* are the differences that matter, and how can capitalists address them? Because of its contrasts with life at large, the Clubhouse Village model serves well as a reference point for purported demonstrations that capitalism across society is not feasible and/or desirable, since it seems eminently feasible and desirable in the Clubhouse Village.

II

THE PRINCIPLES REALIZED IN THE CLUBHOUSE VILLAGE

The moral principles realized in the Clubhouse Village include the principle of voluntary community, the principle of mutual respect, the principle of reciprocity, the principle of social justice, and the principle of beneficence. There are a number of other capitalist principles with which the Clubhouse Village, as I have described it, complies. Here I shall only illustrate a few such principles.

The *first principle* realized is what we might call the *principle of voluntary community*. This principle holds that people should live and cooperate with one another without resorting to violence or threats of violence. It thus holds that all should have the "freedom to communicate, to be, to go, to love, and to do what [they] love without the imposition of others."[11] Under this ideal, all interactions are based on respect and consent. No one is coerced or threatened into behaving well or cooperating with others. Villagers do not need violence to induce good behavior. Villagers are free to come and go. They are not coerced into social life—they are there as volunteers, not conscripts.

Now, in our own world, unlike in the village, we often back up certain rules with threats. Our governments produce innumerable rules and regulations. Breaking these rules comes at a cost. The government may fine us, jail us, or even kill us if we resist. We similarly make threats against one another. We let it be known that we will fight back if attacked, or will call in the police to fight back for us.

Similarly, in our own world, we often disagree about what justice requires. We turn some of these moral disputes into political disputes. We vote, and then we enforce the outcome of this vote, ultimately, at gunpoint.

But the Mickey Mouse Clubhouse Village dispenses with the threats of violence that permeate our society. The villagers do the right thing for the right reason. They have no need of political machinery. The villagers are not morally flawed like we are. They know what justice and morality require and then do it because it's right. The few times they have disputes—and the disputes are minor—a quick pep talk about ethics is all it takes to let them see the light. So, for instance, if Donald becomes a bit too competitive during the balloon race, Mickey need only remind him that the point is to have fun.

The *second principle* realized in the village is the *principle of mutual respect*. This principle covers a wide range of behaviors. The villagers are tolerant of one another and their differences in taste and attitudes. This is not merely a "live-and-let-live" kind of tolerance, but an enlightened form of tolerance, in which the villagers take joy in the diversity of life experiences and perspectives the others bring to the table. The villagers lead satisfying lives of their own, but also live vicariously by seeing the other kinds of lives others lead. The diversity of the Clubhouse Village makes everyone's life all the richer.

The villagers allow each other the freedom to pursue their respective visions of the good life. They do not interfere in one another's projects. This does not mean they are aloof, diffident, or standoffish, of course. They are always willing to lend each other a hand.

In the Mickey Mouse Clubhouse Village, villagers are free to speak their minds, worship or not worship as they choose, work and own businesses as they please, and love whomever they wish, so long as they do not violate others' rights. So, for instance, while many countries in our own world at one time forbade interracial marriage, no Clubhouse Villager condemns the romance between Goofy Dawg and Clarabelle Cow.

Part of what it means to have mutual respect is to believe that every individual matters as an end in herself. While the villages are happy to use their talents for others' good, and in that sense they see everyone's talents as a common bounty, they would never sacrifice one another for the collective. This is much different from our world, in which we often see each other as tools to be exploited for collective ends. They do not see each other as eggs which must be broken if we are to make omelets.

The *third principle* realized on the trip is the principle of reciprocity. While the villagers always pitch in to help with others' misfortune (as I will explain below), they do not primarily confront each other as creatures of need. Rather, they trade value for value with one another in all of their relationships.

To say that the villagers live by trade may make it sound as though they are cunning, calculating people, trying to get what they can for themselves, just like the selfish people we see in real-life societies, such as communist Cuba or the Democratic People's Republic of Korea.

Not so. Clubhouse Villagers are proud of what they have to offer one another. They are proud that each of them is a net benefit to the society they live in and to the others with whom they interact. They are proud that the Clubhouse Village is better off with them than without them. They each have something to offer—not by luck, but because they continually choose to make themselves the kinds of beings who have something to offer.

The villagers produce in part because productivity is an excellence. They produce in part because they have a spirit of commitment. They get satisfaction from being able to serve each other. They serve, and they wish to be served in turn, but they do not serve only in order to be served.

The villagers thus display massive civic virtue, where civic virtue is the disposition and ability to serve the common good. They recognize that by specializing in different tasks and trading, they can create an extended system of cooperation that makes it more likely that each of them can achieve their conception of the good life. They are disposed to give as they take. Each of them profits from their life in the village, but the village also profits from each of them. They have crafted their society into what economists would call a "positive-sum game," that is, a society in which all participants are winners.

This brings us to the *fourth principle* that the villagers realize, the *principle of social justice*. That is, they live under a set of rules designed to ensure that no one, through no fault of his or her own, will lead a less than decent life. The norms of trade, private property, respect, and so on, ensure that everyone has sufficient opportunity, wealth, and freedom to have a good chance to live out his or her individual conception of the good.

In our own world, we often try to achieve such goals through coercion—by having governments control and provide services, or by having governments tax the successful to transfer resources to the less fortunate. And perhaps, under our dire circumstances, the villagers might be willing to accept such brutal, direct, and antisocial methods of achieving social justice. However, the villagers prefer a kinder, indirect, and pro-social way of achieving social justice. The villagers dispense with the State and instead use the institutions of civil society to achieve their ends. They also rely upon spontaneous order—that is, with the right background institutions, good outcomes emerge as a byproduct of everyone's small-scale interactions, with no need for a planner or overseer to coordinate everything.

Finally, the *fifth principle* of the village is a *principle of beneficence*. Villagers are always willing to help those in need. They care about one another, and, where necessary and possible, care for one another, and, too, care that they care about one another.

The villagers do not make themselves objects of charity by choice—that would violate the spirit of reciprocity. However, they sometimes suffer from unexpected bad luck, including many bizarre events they could never reasonably anticipate, such as crash landing on Mars, getting a wicked case of the hiccups shortly before a show, or having to chase a ball that won't stop bouncing. The villagers always come together to ensure that any such crisis is resolved.

This doesn't mean they are suckers to be exploited. If, say, Pete acted like a dishonest socialist, and were to pretend to have a cold in order to get some of Minnie's minestrone soup, Mickey and Minnie would call him out on his fib.

In the Clubhouse Village, there may be differences in wealth. Clarabelle seems to own many different stores, while Donald does not. She may be ten or ten thousand times as rich as Donald. Not everything is held in common. But, unlike in our world, where people constantly compare themselves to others, the villagers do not mind. They have no thirst for material equality. They do not suffer from the socially destructive emotion of envy. (Even less would they attempt to sanitize it to build an ideology around it.) So, while there may be differences in wealth, this does not interfere with their community spirit, their friendship, their common experiences together, or their ability to love and empathize with one another. For them, this is just another difference—in the same way that Donald is a better dancer than Goofy or that Minnie has more common sense than Daisy. It does not drive them apart. This is unlike our world, in which some people are so envious and resentful of others' good fortune that they could not form a community with those richer than themselves, and in which some people are so supercilious and lacking in empathy that they cannot form a community with those much poorer than themselves.

Remember that while the villagers are benevolent and beneficent, they do not *force* one another to act beneficently. While they are happy to undertake personal sacrifices for the sake of the common good or for others, they would not dare *force* one another to undertake such sacrifices. In their view, each villager possesses "an inviolability, founded on justice, that even the welfare of society as a whole cannot override."[12] While they all see themselves as having duties to aid one another, and while they all gladly help one another, they also each affirm that each of them has the right to exist for his or her own sake.

These five principles are in some deep sense anti-socialist. Under socialism, we have seen, there is mutuality, but this is only a by-product of a fundamentally non-reciprocating attitude. The immediate motive toward productivity in a socialist society is (not always but typically) some mixture of fear and greed in proportions that vary with the details of the person's political position and personal character. It is true that people can and do engage in socialist activity under other inspirations (some positive, such as genuine altruism; some negative, such as the desire to dominate others), but the motives of greed and fear are what socialist societies bring to prominence, and that includes greed on behalf of, and fear for the safety of, one's family.

Even when one has wider concerns than one's mere self, the socialist position is greedy and fearful in that one's fellow socialist citizens are predominantly seen at best as possible sources of enrichment at best and at worst as threats or mouths to feed. These are horrible ways of seeing other people, however much we have become habituated and inured to them after a century of socialist civilization.

In the USSR, Venezuela, or Cuba, cooperation is based largely on greed and fear. A person does not care *fundamentally*, within socialist interaction, about how well or badly anyone other than herself fares. They cooperate with other people not because they believe cooperating is a good thing in itself, not because they want all people to flourish, but because they seek to gain and they know that they can do so only if they cooperate with others, or because they worry they will be imprisoned if they do not do as they are told. In the mutual provisioning of a socialist society, we are essentially indifferent to the fate of the farmer whose food we eat: there is little or no community, respect, or beneficence among us, as those values were articulated above. In this kind of system, what we tend to find is that the people pretend to work and the government pretends to pay.

III

IS THE IDEAL DESIRABLE?

Capitalists aspire to realize the principles that structure life in the Mickey Mouse Clubhouse Village on an international scale. Capitalists face two distinct questions, which are often not treated as distinctly as they should be. The first is: would capitalism, if feasible, be desirable? The second is: is capitalism feasible?

Some might say that the Mickey Mouse Clubhouse Village is itself unattractive, that, as matter of principle, there should be *scope* for much greater political control of other people, even in this small-scale village, than the village permits. Now, these opponents are unlikely to say that there *should* be less community, mutual respect, reciprocity, social justice, or beneficence. Rather, they assert that the collective should have a right to make choices for the individuals that form part of that collective. These people might say that in capitalist societies, each individual's choices are already constrained by others' choices. The choices available to each of us are a consequence of everyone else's individual choices. These opponents simply prefer that the restrictions we face result from the conscious deliberation of the collective—or whoever speaks for that collective—rather than be the by-product of everyone's individual choices.

These opponents aside, many others would instead say that while it is all right for the Mickey Mouse Clubhouse Village to be run on capitalist lines, there are features special to the Clubhouse Village that distinguish it from the normal life in a modern society and that consequently cast doubt on the desirability and/or feasibility of realizing Mickey Mouse Clubhouse principles in a modern society. Such people might grant that I have displayed the attractiveness, and the feasibility, of capitalist values, but only in the course of an isolated village, in which there are no competing social groups, and in which everyone to whom the villagers relate is known to them personally and observed by them daily, and in which an individual's family ties exert no counterpull to his sense of social obligation. To what extent do these differences render the ideal undesirable, or less desirable? And to what extent do they render it impracticable?

I do not see that the stated differences between the Mickey Mouse Clubhouse Village and the real world undermine the desirability across society of Clubhouse Village values. I do not think that the cooperation, kindness, freedom, social justice, and respect that the village displays are appropriate only among friends, or within a small community.

In the next section, I address the question of whether it is feasible to instantiate the capitalist values of the Mickey Mouse Clubhouse Village worldwide. But, it seems clear that all people of goodwill would welcome that news that it had become possible to instantiate such values, perhaps, for example, because some economists had invented clever ways of harnessing and organizing our capacity for respect, tolerance, and generosity.

I continue to find appealing the sentiment of a libertarian song I learned in my childhood, which begins as follows: "And the men who hold high places, must be the ones who start, to mold a new reality, closer to the heart, closer to the heart."[13] The point is often made, in resistance to the sentiment of the song, that one cannot be friends with the billions of people who compose our large international society: that the idea is at best impossible to realize, and, so some add, it is even incoherent, because of the exclusivity that goes with friendship. But this song need not be interpreted in that fashion. General social friendship—community—is not an all or nothing thing. It is surely a welcome thing when there is more rather than less community present in society.

But whatever we may wish to conclude about the *desirability* of capitalism, we must also address the question of its *feasibility*, to which I now turn.

IV
IS THE IDEAL FEASIBLE? ARE THE OBSTACLES TO IT HUMAN SELFISHNESS, OR POOR SOCIAL TECHNOLOGY?

Whether or not the capitalist relations of the Mickey Mouse Clubhouse Village are attractive, and whether or not it would also be desirable for such relations to spread across society as a whole, many people who have thought about the matter have judged capitalism to be *infeasible* for society as whole. "Capitalism in one small village, maybe. But capitalism across society? You gotta be kidding!" The idea is that the Mickey Mouse Clubhouse Village is a small village, inhabited by unusually virtuous characters, removed from the complexities of everyday life. It is almost by definition a special place. This kind of society seems implausible on a grand scale.

It is worth pointing out, to begin with, that it is not only in happy contexts, but in much less benign ones, that Clubhouse Village attitudes tend to prevail. People regularly act like Clubhouse Villagers and help each other during emergencies like floods or fires. But let us look at the question of the feasibility of capitalism more closely.

There are two contrasting reasons why society-wide capitalism might be thought infeasible. It is very important, both intellectually and politically, to distinguish them. The first reason has to do with the limits of human nature, and the second has to do with the limits of social technology.

The first putative reason why capitalism is infeasible is that people, so it is often said, are insufficiently cooperative, generous, tolerant, and respectful to meet its requirements, however cooperative, generous, tolerant, and respectful they might be in contexts as special and limited in the Mickey Mouse Clubhouse Village. The second putative reason why capitalism is infeasible is that, even if people were, or could become, in the right culture, sufficiently cooperative, generous, tolerance, and respectful, we do not know how to harness these virtues; we do not know how, through appropriate rules and stimuli, to make these virtues turn the wheels of the economy. Contrast that with human selfishness, fear, and malice, which our experiences in socialist societies show we know how to harness fairly well.

Of course, even if neither of these problems, and no comparable ones, obtained, capitalism might still be unobtainable, because political and ideological forces—including the enormous practical force of the belief that capitalism is infeasible—that would resist a movement toward capitalism are too strong. But the question I am addressing is *not* whether capitalism is straightforwardly *accessible*, whether we can get to it from where we are, and burdened as we are with the massive legacy of socialism, of extractive, predatory, and rent-seeking democracies, and with all the other contingencies that compose our current social condition. The present feasibility question is instead about whether capitalism would work, and be stable, if we were indeed in a position to institute it. And an important aspect of that question is whether the working of a capitalist society would reinforce, or rather, undermine, the cooperative, trustful, and respectful preferences that are required for capitalism's stability.

In my view, the principal problem that the capitalist ideal faces is that we do not know how to design that machinery that would make it run. The problem is not, primarily, human selfishness or malice, but our lack of a suitable organizational technology: our problem is a problem of *design*. It may turn out to be an *insoluble* design problem, and it is a design problem no doubt exacerbated by our selfish, predatory, and malicious propensities, but a design problem, I think, is what we've got.

Both sets of propensities—the set of selfish, predatory, and malicious propensities, but also the set of cooperative, respectful, and generous propensities—reside, after all, in almost everyone. Our problem is that, while we know—as our experience in Russia, Cuba, or Cambodia shows—how to make economic systems work, however badly, on the basis of the development, indeed, the hypertrophy, of selfishness and malice, we do not know how to make economic systems work by developing and exploiting human kindness, generosity, reciprocity, or cooperativeness. Yet even in the real world, a great deal depends on kindness, respect, and generosity, or, to put it generally and more negatively, on non-socialist incentives. Businesspeople, doctors, factory workers, and so on, do not comprehensively gauge what they do in their jobs according to the amount of power and control over others they're likely to get as a result, in the way that politicians or socialist revolutionaries do. (The aforementioned people won't, of course, work for nothing, but the important point here is that they have a mix of motives. They care about making a positive difference in the world, about living lives they consider worthwhile, and about setting an example for their children.)

Yet many political scientists say that once we move past the confines of a small village, like the Clubhouse Village, we cannot make do without a powerful central authority that maintains a powerful police force and military, which imposes rules through commands, backs up these commands through violence and threats of violence, and maintains a monopoly on the use of violence as a method of social control. The thought here is that outside of the confines of a small village, it becomes impossible to develop and set rules without such authorities grounded in violence. While a small village of people who see each other face to face and who have common concern might be able to use social, personal methods to develop rules and maintain compliance to those rules, a large-scale society needs to use anti-social, impersonal methods, such as the coercive nation-state ("the State"). One reason why the village can easily make do without a State is that the information the villagers need to live together peacefully is easy to obtain and aggregate on such a small scale.

Now, the State serves two logically distinguishable functions: a *coordinating* function and an *enforcement* function. First, it makes known to people what the rules are, and thereby allows people to form certain mutual expectations of one another and to plan for the future. But, distinctly, the State also serves as a motivator to people: the threat of violence motivates some people to comply with useful social rules. These two functions are logically separable: sometimes the first operates without the second, as when a person who could get away with a crime chooses not to.

In light of the infirmities of cooperative, non-violent anarchism on one hand, and of the historical injustices visited upon people by the State and the moral shabbiness of political motivation on the other, we should ask whether there might be some means to preserve the coordinating function of the State, to continue to get the benefits it provides of creating useful rules by which we can form long-term plans and mutual expectations, but at the same time extinguish the State's normal motivational presuppositions and distributive consequences. Can we have State efficiency in the production of useful social rules without State incentives, and, hence, without creating a hierarchy in which some people lord over others?

Precisely that distinction is at the center of a groundbreaking book by Michael Huemer, who works in the Philosophy Department at the University of Colorado. The book, published in 2013, was called *The Problem of Political Authority: An Examination of the Right to Coerce and the Duty to Obey*. Huemer describes a society in which market-based firms provide protection and resolve disputes non-violently, without the need to create powerful entrenched bureaucracies or politicians who lord over the rest of us. Laws could arise through agreements and contracts rather than by legislative fiat, much as the merchant law of Renaissance-era Europe developed and was maintained without state support.

There are plenty of problems with the Huemer scheme, but it seems to me to be one that is amply worth refining. The principles behind the scheme enjoy a modest measure of realization whenever people with the opportunity to cheat or prey upon one another choose not to do so on moral grounds, or whenever people find a way to create and maintain social order without having to call in the police.

Less ambitious but similarly groundbreaking are works by Robert Nozick (a philosopher from Harvard University and author of *Anarchy, State, and Utopia*) and John Tomasi (a political theorist at Brown University and author of *Free Market Fairness*). Nozick and Tomasi both describe how relatively limited or "minimal" states could provide coordinating functions in creating and enforcing certain laws. However, unlike contemporary nation-states, in which special interest groups compete to use the apparatus of the State to prey upon others, these minimal states keep their hands off the economy, and thus greatly reduce the predatory rent-seeking to which we are accustomed. Tomasi also argues that if private charity is not enough, his still quite-minimal state can provide certain forms of social insurance.

Now, none of these schemes fully satisfy the capitalist standards of morality that are realized in the Mickey Mouse Clubhouse Village. Huemer's coercive private enforcement agency capitalism and Nozick and Tomasi's minimal-state capitalism remain deficient, from the capitalist point of view, because there is always a moral failing in a society in which some people hold positions of coercive power over others or in which some people threaten to wield violence against others. The use of such violence tends against the value of community.

Could we go even further than Tomasi, Nozick, or Huemer toward a capitalist direction? I do not know whether the needed refinements are possible, nor do I know, speaking more generally, whether the full capitalist ideal is feasible. We capitalists don't *now* know how to replicate Mickey Mouse Clubhouse Village procedures on a nation-wide or greater scale, amid the complexity and variety that comes with size. We don't *now* know how to give a regime of both separate and communal ownership, reciprocity, beneficence, and respect the real meaning that it has in the Clubhouse Village but which it doesn't have in the United States and in similarly ordered states. We do not know how to instantiate such values on a large scale. But—but!—I do not think we now *know* for sure that we will never know how to do these things: I am agnostic on that score. Perhaps in the distant future, with advances in human moral motivation and social technology, the principles of the Mickey Mouse Clubhouse Village could be realized.

The technology for using base motives for productive and coordinating effects is reasonably well understood. Indeed, the history of the past few hundred years encourages the thought that the easiest way to generate order and social coordination in a modern society is by nourishing the motives of which I spoke earlier, namely, those of greed, fear, and the lust for power.

But we should never forget that greed, fear, and the lust for power are repugnant motives. Who would propose running a society on the basis of such motives, and thereby promoting the psychology to which they belong, if they were not known to be effective, if they did not have the instrumental value which is the only value they have? James Madison said the secret to working political structures is that ambition must be made to counteract ambition. Or, take a more mundane source, an economics textbook by Greg Mankiw: "There are two broad reasons for a government to intervene in an economy and change the allocation of resources that people would choose on their own: to promote efficiency or to promote equality. That is, most policies aim either to enlarge the economic pie or change how the pie is divided."[14] Madison and Mankiw thereby propound a wholly instrumental justification of political and socialist motivation, in the face of their unattractive intrinsic character.

Old-style capitalists often forget Madison's or Mankiw's points—they begin with a moralistic condemnation of the State or of socialist institutions that fails to address their instrumental justification. Certain contemporary capitalists, tend, contrariwise, to forget that the State is intrinsically repugnant, because they are blinded by their belated discovery of the State's instrumental value. It is the genius of the State and of socialist institutions that they (1) recruit low-grade motives to (2) desirable ends; but (3) they also produce undesirable effects; including significant unjust malevolence, predation, and war. In a balanced view, all three sides of that proposition must be kept in focus, but many statist capitalists now self-deceptively overlook (1) and (3). As George Washington is rumored to have said, "Government is not reason; it is not eloquence—it is force. Like fire, it is a dangerous servant and a fearful master."[15] Yet many contemporary celebrants of the State play down this truth.

V
CODA

Any attempt to realize the capitalist ideal runs up against entrenched socialist power and individual human selfishness and malice. Politically serious people must take these obstacles seriously. But they are *not* reason to disparage the ideal itself. Disparaging the ideal because it faces those obstacles leads to confusion, and confusion generates disoriented practice: there are contexts in which this ideal *can* be advanced, but is pushed forward less resolutely than it might be because of a lack of clarity about what the ideal is.

The capitalist aspiration is to extend community, respect, reciprocity, social justice, and beneficence to the whole of our economic life. As I have acknowledged, we now know that we do not know how to do that, and many think we now know that it is impossible to do that. It is imperative now to defend these values, as they are currently under aggressive threat by socialists.

The natural tendency of the socialist state is to increase the scope of the social relations that it covers, because political entrepreneurs see opportunities to secure special privileges and rents at the end to turn what is not yet controlled collectively through force into something that is. Left to its own, the socialist dynamic is self-sustaining, and capitalists therefore need the power of organized politics to oppose it: their socialist opponents, who go with the grain of the system, need that power less (which is not to say that they lack it!).

Capitalism is an attempt to get beyond the predatory phrase of human development. Every socialist society, she says, is a system of predation. Our attempts to get beyond predation have thus far failed. I do not think the right conclusion is to give up.

This completes my parody of Cohen's *Why Not Socialism?*. I mostly took Cohen's own arguments but reversed the words. Oddly, it works better as a defense of capitalism than Cohen's own defense of socialism. Over the next two chapters, I explain what this all means for the debate.

Three

G. A. Cohen says we should not rest content with what we have. We can envision a better world free of oppression. We should strive to achieve that vision, if we can. I agree.

But I think Cohen's ultimate legacy will be—contrary to his intentions—to help us see that this best possible world is capitalist, not socialist. Capitalism is not just better than socialism from an economic point of view, but inherently better from a moral point of view.

I doubt socialist readers were convinced by the Mickey Mouse Clubhouse argument in Chapter 2. They might—should!—suspect there is something dubious about the argument there. It was indeed a kind of philosophical prestidigitation. But though the argument is flawed, I purposefully constructed to copy the flaws of Cohen's own argument. The difference between Cohen and me, here, is that I know it's flawed.

That said, we are about to do some *real* magic. When we combine (1) Cohen's flawed argument for the intrinsic moral superiority of socialism, and (2) my almost-as-flawed argument for the intrinsic moral superiority of capitalism, with (3) a little reflection on what went wrong, what emerges is (4) a *good* argument for the intrinsic moral superiority of capitalism.

In this chapter, I begin by explaining what Cohen is trying to accomplish, and why his argument is fallacious. In the

DOI: 10.4324/9781003424116-3

next chapter, I argue that even if everyone were morally perfect, capitalism would still be preferable to socialism.

NOT THE ISSUE: DOES HUMAN NATURE IMPOSE LIMITS ON JUSTICE?

Cohen has a diagnosis of why political philosophy goes wrong—why, in his view, political philosophers are too sanguine about markets and capitalism. *Why Not Socialism?* is a small piece of Cohen's broader project to rescue philosophy from its errant ways. Cohen thinks philosophers have constructed unambitious theories of justice because they mistakenly treat defects in human motivation as a constraint on justice. In particular, Cohen thinks philosophers mistakenly treat facts about what people are willing to do as a constraint on what people ought to do.

To understand Cohen's complaint, we need some background on the philosopher John Rawls. (Unfortunately, in my opinion,) the most important and influential book of political philosophy in the past hundred years is John Rawls's *A Theory of Justice*. Rawls's critic Robert Nozick, also one of the most important political philosophers of the past century, went so far as to say, "Political philosophers must now work within Rawls's theory or say why not."[1] Cohen's final book before his death—*Rescuing Justice and Equality*—was meant to explain why we should *not* work within Rawls's theory. In fact, Cohen says, we need to *rescue* philosophy from Rawls's way of thinking. Rawls is blinding us to what justice really is.

Cohen claims that the problem with Rawls (and with most other political philosophers, thanks to Rawls's influence) is that Rawls permits sad facts about human motivation to constrain what count as principles of justice. Cohen thinks that this largely explains why Rawls and Nozick defend market-based economies, while Cohen defends socialism. According to Cohen, Rawls, Nozick, and most other political philosophers dumb down their theories of justice to accommodate people's weak moral motivations. But if Rawls and others realized that that's a mistake, then they would see that justice requires socialism and equality.

Rawls's theorizing about justice starts with the idea that society is a cooperative venture for mutual gain. In society, we have both congruence and conflicts of interest. We have congruence, because each of us has a stake in society and the institutions we live under. But there are conflicts, because we each would prefer a bigger rather than a smaller share of whatever goods society has to offer.

Justice, Rawls says, is meant to resolve these conflicts. Justice is about securing fair terms of cooperation. But what count as fair terms?

Consider all the factors in a normal market society that tend to cause some people to do better than others. Many of these factors are nothing more than luck, Rawls says. For instance, children from Northwest DC tend to have much better life prospects than children from Southwest DC, in part because the parents in Northwest DC are richer, better educated, and have more social and human capital. But it is not as though any of these children did anything to deserve being born to rich or poor parents. It's all luck.

Or, to take another example, in 2013 *People* magazine declared actress Gwyneth Paltrow the most beautiful woman in the world. Paltrow's beauty helped make her rich. But Paltrow is beautiful in large part because she won the genetic lottery. She inherited good genes from her beautiful parents. Sure, Paltrow exercises and eats well, but even with the same diet and exercise, the average woman would not be as beautiful as Paltrow. Thus, the average woman is cut off from most of the opportunities Paltrow enjoys. Therefore, a great part of Paltrow's success is luck.

And so, Rawls complains—and Cohen complains with him—one problem with our society is that some people do much better than others on morally arbitrary grounds. Rawls and Cohen both believe that inequalities resulting from mere luck are at least presumptively unjust. As I explained in Chapter 1, Cohen often claims that perfectly just people would not allow *any* inequality to result from pure luck.

But Rawls disagrees. Rawls thinks the presumption against allowing luck-based inequality can be overcome. Rawls argues that the fair terms of social cooperation would be whatever principles people would agree to in a hypothetical bargaining situation known as the "original position." In the original position, the bargainers are asked to pick principles of justice that will govern the society in which they will live. The bargainers are rational, so they pick rules from which they expect to benefit. They are not envious, so they seek to maximize how well they do in absolute, rather than relative, terms. However, to make sure they pick *fair* rules, the bargainers are placed under a "veil of ignorance." While they know general facts about what human beings are like, the veil of ignorance prevents them from knowing facts about themselves, such as their race, gender identity, sex, conception of the good life, religion, personal abilities, relative position in society, what their parents will be like, and so on. It also prevents them from knowing what the probabilities are that will have any particular characteristics. So, for instance, bargainers not only don't know whether they will be white or black, but they also don't know the probability that they will be white or black. This veil of ignorance thus prevents the bargainers from picking principles that advantage themselves at everyone else's expense. Instead, because they do not know their particular identities, they will pick principles that are to *everyone's* advantage. Self-interested, rational, non-envious bargainers under a veil of ignorance will pick rules that tend to make everyone in society a winner.

At one point in their deliberation, the bargainers consider how to divide up the fruits of social cooperation. Their first thought is that they should distribute everything equally. To see why, imagine we came across a tasty unowned pie. The most intuitive way to split it would be to give everyone an equal slice. However, suppose it turns out to be a magic pie. That is, suppose that the pie changes *size* depending on how we cut it. If we cut it equally, the pie stays small. But, if we cut unequally, the pie becomes much bigger. Rawls says that if we are rational and not envious, we will all prefer to cut the pie such that we get *unequal but bigger* slices rather than *equally small* slices.

And so, Rawls argues, the bargainers in the original position will pick principles of justice that allow inequality, provided inequality causes everyone to get a bigger slice. The bargainers realize that by rewarding certain people for being unusually productive or talented, everyone can be better off. It is to everyone's advantage to live by rules under which a Steve Jobs or Warren Buffett can accumulate more wealth than less talented, ambitious, or conscientious people. Once we realize that the size of the pie depends upon people making that pie, we want to encourage pie-making.[2] This holds true even if a large part of Jobs's and Buffett's talent is luck—winning the genetic lottery.

Cohen thinks Rawls's argument is morally bogus. He says Rawls makes the fundamental mistake of allowing *ignoble* human motivations to constrain the content of our theories of justice. Now, when it comes to making practical policy in the real world, Cohen concurs with Rawls that if the only way to motivate people to work hard is to pay them greater-than-normal rewards, we might give in and allow some inequality. But, Cohen admonishes us, don't call the resulting inequality *just*! Making concessions to unjust motivations, under conditions of duress, might be the best we can do, but it's not justice.

Rawls says that inequality is justified only if it is necessary to help improve everyone's lot. But, Cohen claims, Rawls's argument for allowing inequality only works if we assume people are selfish. However, Cohen says, in a perfectly just society, all people are committed to achieving justice. This means that the most talented people will themselves affirm the view that inequality is justified only if it is necessary to improve everyone's lot. If so, then the most talented people wouldn't say, "We should allow inequality because we, the talented, refuse to work hard and use our talents well unless we get paid more." If the talented refused to work hard without getting paid extra, that would show they weren't committed to Rawls's principles of justice. But Rawls says that a just society is one in which everyone is committed to realizing justice. Thus, the talented would instead say, "We, the talented, being committed to justice, will simply choose to work hard and make good use of our talents without having to get paid more. Therefore, it's not necessary to pay us more, and so inequality is not necessary or justified." In a just society, people have good moral motivations. And if people had *good* moral motivations, they would be willing to work hard and use their talents for the common good without having to be bribed. Cohen thinks Rawls's *Theory of Justice* isn't really a theory of *justice* at all.

Recall that Cohen already illustrated this point with the socialist camping trip. Harry and Leslie are unusually talented at catching fish and cracking nuts. They were willing to make use of their talents only if they would become richer than the other campers. Cohen agrees that in such circumstances, we might decide that it's worth paying off Harry and Leslie so that we can all get more fish and nuts. But Harry and Leslie are still being selfish, callous jerks. If Harry and Leslie had genuine fellow-feeling, community spirit, and a strong sense of justice, they would be willing to catch fish and crack nuts for the sake of everyone, without demanding extra payment.

Remember, Cohen is not saying that Harry and Leslie should become everyone's slaves just because they are more talented. He is not claiming that talented people should work extra hard for the sake of idle people. Rather, he's saying that in a just world, everyone should work equally hard, and everyone should get an equal share, regardless of differences in talent.

Thanks to Cohen's critique of Rawls, one of the major debates in political philosophy is to what degree, if any, facts about human nature constrain what count as the correct principles of justice.[3] According to Cohen, Rawls allows the fact that people are selfish to justify allowing inequalities in wealth and opportunity. But, Cohen says, even if such inequalities should be allowed all things considered, this is the devil's bargain. Cohen concludes that facts about *what people are willing to do* are no constraint at all upon the principles of justice.[4]

The philosopher Peter Singer makes similar arguments about our duties of charity. Singer argues that we have a moral obligation to spend money saving lives rather than spending money on luxury goods.[5] After all, Singer says, from a moral point of view, it's clearly more important for me to save a life than for me to drive an Infiniti sports car.[6] Singer's views are extremely demanding. Singer doesn't just mean that you should save a life rather than buy an Infiniti. Rather, for him, a luxury good is anything you don't strictly need. Almost everything you consume is a luxury good so defined—you could have purchased cheaper substitute goods and saved lives with the leftover money.

Now, hardly anyone lives up to Singer's principles. Even Singer himself—who says he donates 20% of his income to charity—falls short. (Singer is one the richest people in the world and could give much more.) But, Singer says, that's because we—Singer included—are all too selfish. None of us have strong enough moral motivation. Morality does not demand of us more than we *can* do, but it does demand more than we *want* to do. But so what? The fact that we are selfish and callous has no bearing on what morality requires.

In *Utopophobia*,[7] David Estlund rigorously examines the circumstances under which people's attitudes and motivations constitute genuine barriers that block or otherwise relieve them of what would have been motivations. He argues that these circumstances are highly constrained.

Estlund argues that positing human selfishness typically adds nothing in estimating people's moral requirements. Bill might be too selfish to clean up his mess, but that does not excuse him. His selfishness does not explain away his obligations; rather, it explains *why* he fails to meet his obligations.[8] If most people are too selfish to clean up the messes they impose on others, it does not follow that they have no obligation to clean. It follows instead that most people act badly because they are selfish.[9]

Estlund notes that conflicting motives might sometimes appear to override our obligations, but upon further inspection, it's not the motives, but *other obligations*, that are doing the work. For instance, imagine that if a psychiatrist divulges her patients' medical secrets, this will somehow promote socially just outcomes. Suppose the psychiatrist is nevertheless strongly motivated to keep the secrets. Here, Estlund agrees that the psychiatrist lacks a duty to promote social justice by divulging secrets. But the reason is not her unwillingness, per se, but rather her preexisting obligations to her clients—obligations that enjoy lexical priority over the demands of social justice.[10]

Estlund also warns us not to confuse questions of personal moral prerogative with questions of motivation. Many theorists argue that individuals have a wide sphere of personal prerogative to live their lives as they see fit; they are not required to dedicate their entire lives to promoting utilitarian ends, human welfare, or social justice.[11] Though Estlund officially remains neutral about the content of morality and justice in *Utopophobia*, he accepts that personal prerogative might block what otherwise would have been duties to act in certain ways. For instance, perhaps Estlund would have better served social justice by becoming a medical researcher, but personal prerogative permits him to be a philosopher. However, Estlund contends, the justification for thinking people have such personal prerogative is not that people are callous, selfish, or unwilling to do what's right. Rather, personal prerogative is grounded in people's legitimate interests in living a free and autonomous life of their own design. Once again, Estlund concludes, "I don't want to do that" is not itself a justification for thinking, "I have no duty to do that."

Estlund claims that contrary motives block obligations only in special cases, only when the motive is "clinical." For instance, if a person genuinely cannot choose to do something due to some genuine psychological disability, the obligation is blocked. Estlund allows that if a person could choose to do something, but due to a psychological condition, doing so would impose severe hardship, then the person may be excused. For instance, a person might normally be obligated to pull a child from a well, but is at least partly excused if she has severe phobia of enclosed spaces and the dark.[12]

Overall, Estlund claims, we must be careful not to assume that contrary motives are disabling. Otherwise, we cast people as if they lacked the appropriate kind of free will or moral agency. Rich could give to Poor, even though he'd much rather buy a yacht. People could avoid cheating or free riding on public goods, even though they are tempted to cheat. People could work for others' benefit without expecting a selfish return, even though they're callous. Business owners could play fair and avoid shady practices, even though they are tempted to snatch illicit profits.[13] Appealing to contrary motives, such as wealth, status, self-interest, bias, leisure, love, or fear does not block a moral obligation, Estlund says, unless the person is genuinely disabled by these motives. Further, it does not matter for Estlund whether these motives result from human nature or poor socialization.

For some reason, when discussing the limits of our duties of charity and beneficence, many people are inclined to disagree with Singer, Estlund, or Cohen about whether what we are willing to do constrains what we ought to do. In this context, many people think "don't want to" implies, at some point, "don't have to." Yet many of these same people would deny this implication in other contexts, when we are talking about our duties to avoid harming others.

For instance, suppose my moral theory implies that rape is wrong. Now suppose a man—call him Albert—says, "Oh, no, you don't understand. I very much *want* to commit rape. I refuse not to rape women. I thus find your moral theory *too demanding*." No one would think that this excuses Albert or permits him to rape. He finds the moral duty not to rape demanding not because it really does demand too much of him, but because he is a vile person. Now, psychologists and criminologists might determine that that it is unrealistic to expect a world free of rape. Perhaps there will always be people like Albert, who want to rape. Still, that has no bearing on whether rape is permissible. Rape remains wrong.

Similarly, suppose a political philosopher says, "Governments should follow the rules of just war theory, which forbids governments from initiating aggressive conflicts." Now, pessimist that I am, I doubt there will come a time when all governments follow the rules of just war. If they did, after all, there would be no war at all. Still, that has little bearing on whether they should or should not follow the rules of just war. People in governments could easily act better, but many don't *want* to do so. The predominant reason that governments in the past have violated the standards of just war is that people—kings, presidents, generals, senators, soldiers on the ground, and, yes, democratic voters[14]—have been callous, cruel, power-hungry, nationalistic, or culpably incompetent and misinformed. A secondary reason is that many think they must act this way because otherwise other callous, cruel, power-hungry people will depose them. (For instance, perhaps leaders in Russia think they must act like Putin lest would-be Putins will kill and replace them.)

Cohen thinks this is where the action is in current political philosophy. Cohen advocates radical socialism and radical equality, while Rawls's theory of justice allows for capitalist markets and significant inequality.[15] Cohen thinks the reason Rawls's theory allows for markets and inequality is just that Rawls illicitly compromises with vile, selfish human nature. But, Cohen claims, once we realize that facts about human selfishness have no bearing on what counts as justice, we will all be socialists and egalitarians. That's what the Camping Trip thought experiment is meant to prove.

Some defenders of markets respond, pace Cohen, that concerns about human motivation *do* constrain our principles of justice. For instance, philosopher David Schmidtz agrees with Cohen that "I am not willing to do X" doesn't imply "I have no duty to do X." However, Schmidtz says, while I can control my own actions, I cannot control what others do. I cannot simply count on them to live by high standards. Schmidtz says justice is about "coping with circumstances where 'won't do' on the part of others entails a descriptive 'can't do' on my part."[16] Cohen claims that justice is what we get when we don't have to worry about whether people will comply with whatever purported principles of justice we advance. Schmidtz says that a lack of compliance is the very problem principles of justice are supposed to solve, not in the sense that principles of justice induce everyone to comply, but rather that principles of justice tell us how to live well together in a world where we cannot take it for granted that others will act well.

Similarly, David Hume says that principles of justice apply only in a world where people are not fully altruistic, but also not so selfish as to be unmoved by moral demands. He calls justice a "jealous, guarded virtue." Hume would deny that justice is realized on Cohen's camping trip or in the Mickey Mouse Clubhouse Village. Instead, he would say that these situations *transcend* the circumstances of justice.

This debate seems to me largely terminological, about whether we want to reserve the word "justice" for ideal societies—where we can imagine human beings have the moral motivations they should have—or whether we want to use "justice" to refer to moral rules it seems reasonable to demand of one another that we live by in the real world—where we know most people will have imperfect motives. Hume, Schmidtz, and Rawls haven't undermined Cohen's assertion that the world Cohen envisions is *better* from a moral point of view. Rather, Hume, Schmidtz, and Rawls seem simply to disagree about whether we should call Cohen's highly demanding socialist principles "principles of justice" or something else.[17]

Unlike most other critics, I want to take Cohen head-on. I grant Cohen that justice is the thing that is realized in utopia, where people are as morally pure as they are in the socialist camping trip or the Mickey Mouse Clubhouse Village. But, contrary to Cohen, even if we play the game of political philosophy on his terms, capitalism, not socialism, wins. Contrary to Cohen, even if the limits of human motivation are not a constraint, we should still advocate capitalism, not socialism. Cohen thinks he can argue for socialism by occupying the moral high ground over Rawls and Nozick. But I have found a morally higher ground for capitalism to occupy.

In this chapter, I explain the two major fallacies present in Cohen's argument. That is, this chapter shows Cohen's argument for socialism fails. In the next chapter, I go on to explain why utopia is capitalist.

THE FIRST COHEN FALLACY: COMPARING IDEAL TO REAL

Cohen argues that socialism is better than capitalism. His argument looks like this:

1. The socialist camping trip was better than the capitalist camping trip.
2. It would be desirable to make the world run like the socialist camping trip—having the world run like the socialist camping trip would be better than the way the world actually is.
3. Therefore, socialism is intrinsically more desirable than capitalism.

The problem is that even if we grant Cohen's premises (1 and 2), his conclusion (3) does not follow.

Cohen asked us to imagine a fictional socialist micro-society in which all the participants are *stipulated* to have (more or less) perfect moral character and behavior, or at least the moral behavior he thinks they are required to have to count as just and good. He then compared this to what he took to be a realistic depiction of capitalism, with some of the nasty behaviors we actually see in real-life capitalism, such as greed, callousness, and status-seeking competitiveness. In the socialist version of the camping trip, he stipulated that the campers were motivated by fellow feeling, community spirit, and love. In the capitalist version, he stipulated that they are selfish and fearful. We all preferred the "socialist" version of the camping trip to the capitalist version. And we would all prefer to live in a world more like the socialist camping trip than like what Cohen calls the capitalist camping trip. And so, Cohen concludes, socialism is intrinsically more desirable than capitalism.

There is something all too easy about his argument. All Cohen did was compare an imaginary, idealized, unrealistic version of a socialist regime to a more realistic version of a capitalist regime. He may be right that his imaginary, idealized, unrealistic socialist regime is better than a realistic capitalist regime. But, even if he is right, this is not very interesting. Cohen's argument is really nothing more than this:

1. Socialism with morally perfect (or at least extremely good) people is better than capitalism with real, flawed people.
2. A world of socialism with morally perfect (or at least extremely good) people is better than our actual world, with real, flawed people.
3. Therefore, socialism is intrinsically more desirable than capitalism.

But obviously 3 doesn't follow from 1 and 2.

The problem is that Cohen is not comparing like to like. As Rawls says, "we must be careful here not to compare the ideal of one conception with the actuality of the other ..."[18] Daniel Shapiro similarly says, "A sound argument for institutional change must avoid jumping between the real and the ideal."[19] It's not that interesting if an idealized version of one type of regime ends up being better than a non-idealized, realistic version of another type of regime.

The general problem looks like this: Suppose institutions X + morally excellent/perfect people are better than institutions Y + realistically flawed people. This doesn't tell us that institutions X are better than Y. What might be doing the work is the quality of people's character.

Suppose I described a realm ruled by an omniscient, omnibenevolent philosopher king, who always knew exactly what to do to promote the common good, and who always wielded his power to promote the common good of the people in the best way possible. Suppose I then compare that to a realistic democracy—like the United States—in which political power is frequently used in incompetent or morally corrupt ways. I then conclude that I've proven that monarchy is inherently better than democracy. You'd see right through that.

Cohen imagined an idealized socialist society made up of morally perfect (or at least excellent) people, and concluded this idealized socialist society is superior to real world capitalism, with realistically imperfect people. Cohen's *Why Not Socialism?* is in that sense a compelling argument that ideal socialism is in certain ways superior to realistic capitalism. But the relevant comparisons are ideal socialism to ideal capitalism, and real socialism to real capitalism. Or, more precisely, the relevant comparison is to ask, for any given level of moral character among the population, how different institutions would function, keeping in mind that the rules of the game might also influence how good people's character is.

Cohen thus fails to consider whether *ideal capitalism* might be superior to ideal socialism. If Cohen wanted to show socialism is intrinsically superior to capitalism, he would need to compare his socialist camping trip to something like the Mickey Mouse Clubhouse Village.

So, let us dub this kind of fallacious reasoning the *First Cohen Fallacy*. The First Cohen Fallacy is the fallacy of concluding that if an idealized version of system X is better than a realistic, flawed version of system Y, this proves that X is inherently superior to Y.

I'll note in passing that Rawls himself routinely commits the First Cohen Fallacy, even though Rawls admonishes us to avoid it. For instance, in both *A Theory of Justice* and *Justice as Fairness: A Restatement*, Rawls argues that certain political-economic regimes could in principle fully realize justice while others cannot. However, if you look carefully, you'll see that when Rawls discusses his favored regimes, he imagines that people have perfectly just motivations, and he explicitly imagines away many of the problems those regimes would face in the real world. However, when Rawls brings up reasons for rejecting his disfavored regimes, he invokes the kinds of problems that would only occur if people had imperfect motivations.

For instance, Rawls knows that in the real world, the social insurance, redistributive, and regulatory institutions he favors would lead to at least some moral hazard and rent seeking. A policy is said to cause "moral hazard" when it induces people to take more risks or make dumb choices, because the policy allows these people to externalize the costs of their decisions onto others. So, for instance, welfare state policies encourage at least some people not to save enough, to have children out of wedlock, and be unemployed instead of taking a job. "Rent seeking" refers to when corporations, unions, or special interest groups lobby the government to manipulate the legal or regulatory environment in their favor. As the Nobel Laureate economist James Buchanan says, "If the government is empowered to grant monopoly rights or tariff protection to one group, at the expense of the general public or of designated losers, it follows that potential beneficiaries will compete for the prize."[20] No one (or at least no serious person) denies that in the real world, welfare states and government intervention into the economy encourage moral hazard and rent seeking. Instead, the informed debate is over just how bad these problems will be, and whether the benefits of certain aspects of the welfare state and government intervention outweigh the costs. However, when Rawls theorizes about what institutions would be just, he simply dismisses these concerns. He is doing "ideal theory," in which we imagine people have a perfect sense of justice, and is thus imagining a world without moral hazard or rent seeking.[21]

Yet, not a page later, Rawls says that certain other regimes he dislikes are unjust because they might encourage people of great wealth to use their wealth to buy government power for their own ends. But, by Rawls's ground rules, we're supposed to be doing ideal theory, and imagining that people have a perfect sense of justice.[22] And if people had a perfect sense of justice, they would not buy government power for their own selfish ends, since by hypothesis this is unjust.

Some Rawlsians might say that Rawls's complaint is not that the system would *cause* people to act unjustly, but that it would *allow* them to do so. But this doesn't save his argument. Rawls's favored institutions similarly *allow* unjust abuses, but he dismisses when doing ideal theory. When Rawls evaluates different regimes as candidates to realize justice as fairness, he cheats.

So, like Cohen, Rawls doesn't play fair. When Rawls argues for one set of institutions over another, he commits the First Cohen Fallacy. It renders his comparative analysis of institutions and regimes worse than useless; into the trash it goes.

THE SECOND COHEN FALLACY: IDENTIFYING REGIMES WITH VALUES OR MOTIVES

Cohen often seems to just identify socialism with a set of moral principles and virtuous dispositions he likes. Political theorist Sharon Krause notices this too:

> the fact that most of us intuitively find a camping trip that is rich in generosity, cooperation, unselfishness, and friendship to be appealing in no way demonstrates that we find socialism, as the collective ownership of property, desirable. It just shows that we value these moral dispositions, as indeed we should. [Cohen's book suffers] from a conceptual ambiguity ... with respect to the meaning of socialism. Sometimes socialism is defined in terms of the specific economic practice of collective ownership; at other times, Cohen equates it with ... equality and community ... and with ... generosity, friendship ... and unselfishness ... Yet nowhere in the book does Cohen demonstrate that collective ownership *uniquely* realizes these general principles and dispositions, or that it is the only way to honor them.[23]

We must be careful not to equate socialism with moral virtue or community spirit. Capitalism and socialism are simply ways of organizing the ownership of property. In capitalism, individuals may own the means of production. In socialism, they may not—the means of production are owned collectively (or by the representative of the collective, such as the State). Socialism is not love or kindness or generosity or oceans of delicious lemonade.[24] Socialism is not equality or community. It's a way of distributing the *control rights* over objects. That's it.

Cohen asserts that capitalism runs on greed and fear. Yet Cohen cannot simply assert this as a conceptual or definitional claim. Capitalism is not analytically tied to greed and fear. Whether a regime is capitalist or not has nothing to do with people's motives. A fearless, greedless capitalist society—like the Mickey Mouse Clubhouse Village—is no less capitalist than a fearful, greedy capitalist society—like Denmark or Switzerland. A social system is capitalist to the extent that it has private property in the means of production, decisions about the use of property are made by owners rather than by governments or society at large, people may make contracts as they please, legal monopolies and subsidies are absent, and so on.

So, if Cohen had said, "By 'capitalism', I just mean a predatory system of greed and fear," that would be no stronger a condemnation of market societies than if Adam Smith said, "By 'socialism', I just mean a system of bloodthirsty dictators who starve and slaughter peasants." We cannot just decide to insert evil motivations into the very definition of capitalism in order to argue that capitalism is evil. That would be both bad philosophy and bad lexicography.

Cohen would respond, I suspect, that we can imagine capitalist economies free of predation, greed, and fear, but real capitalist economies are not free of greed and fear. He would be right. Yet, a defender of capitalism could retort that we can also imagine socialist economies free of greed and fear, but real socialist economies are not free of predation, greed, and fear. Quite the contrary.

Cohen also cannot claim, as some of his defenders say he should (or did), that all he's doing is uncovering the implicit motivations of capitalist societies. Some people have responded to my argument here by claiming that Cohen is instead relying on empirically sound, working sociological approximations of actual institutions. When Cohen says capitalism is a society of greed and fear, he's describing what capitalism is like. But, pace Cohen's defenders, that's not what he's doing. After all, when he describes socialist societies, he doesn't rely on sound, working sociological approximations of actual institutions, but on unrealistic, idealized accounts of how he wants socialism to go.

Cohen claims that actors in market societies are motivated by greed and fear. He is right; many of them are, at least much of the time. And these motives, as well as a host of other moral failings, lead them to do many horrible things in business, government, and private life.

What are people motivated by in socialist societies? In the USSR, Cuba, or Khmer Rouge Cambodia, or in the tens of thousands of failed small-scale socialist experiments in the 1800s, were people motivated by love, generosity, and community? No, they were motivated even more strongly under those regimes by base emotions, such as fear, malice, and the lust for power.

Cohen would say he is not defending the Bolsheviks or the Khmer Rouge, even if he did mourn the passing of the USSR. When he says agents in a socialist society are motivated by community spirit, he is discussing an *imaginary* and *fictional* socialist society. Because Cohen's camping story is fictional, Cohen can simply stipulate that the characters in his story have whatever motivations he likes.

However, notice again how badly this weakens Cohen's argument against capitalism. Cohen says that an advantage of socialism over capitalism is the kind of motivations it engenders and relies upon. When Cohen says that agents in capitalist economies are motivated by greed and fear, he is articulating what he takes to be an empirical generalization about real-life, non-ideal capitalism. When Cohen says that agents in socialist economies are motivated by altruism and community spirit, Cohen is not making an empirical claim at all. Instead, he is simply *stipulating* that the people in his camping trip have good motivations. He is simply stipulating that in his preferred society, people would have nice motives. That's all he's got.

Thus, Cohen is not doing social science. He is not helping us discover what motivates people in different regimes. He is not showing us how different regimes change people's motivations. He is not doing empirical comparative politics or comparative moral psychology. He has not given us any reason whatsoever to believe that socialism engenders or relies upon better motivations than capitalism.

If one really wanted to know what motivates people in market society, one would do genuine social scientific research. One might ask: In the real world, does capitalism encourage predation, greed, fear, poverty, power-grabbing, and other nasty behaviors more so than other kinds of economic systems? What sort of behaviors and attitudes does socialism encourage? These questions cannot be settled by conceptual analysis, stipulation, or imagining people on camping trips. The only way to answer these questions is to go and check, to conduct historical, sociological, and psychological research on what exposure to markets does to people, and what happens when markets are replaced by something else. If capitalism turns out to encourage bad behaviors and bad attitudes, it is to that extent bad. Yet if it also turns out to do so less, in the real world, than the alternatives (such as socialism) do in the real world, then to that extent we have reason to favor capitalism in the real world.

In fact, there are people conducting just this sort of research. Neuroeconomist Paul Zak says:

> market exchange itself may lead to a society where individuals have stronger character values. The clearest evidence for this is the studies of fairness in small-scale societies conducted by Henrich and his colleagues. They showed that *the likelihood of making fair offers to a stranger in one's society is more strongly predicted by the extent of trade in markets than any other factor they have found.* Exchange is inherently other-regarding—both you and I must benefit if exchange is to occur.[25]

Zak says that, as far as the evidence we have goes, market societies induce people to play fair. Economists like to conduct experiments (using large amounts of real money) in which participants have the opportunity to cheat and swindle each other or to play fairly. Joseph Henrich and other researchers have tested a large number of variables to see which factors tend to make people play fair or cheat. Herb Gintis further summarizes these studies:

> Movements for religious and lifestyle tolerance, gender equality, and democracy have flourished and triumphed in societies governed by market exchange, and nowhere else.
>
> My colleagues and I found dramatic evidence of this positive relationship between markets and morality in our study of fairness in simple societies—hunter-gatherers, horticulturalists, nomadic herders, and small-scale sedentary farmers—in Africa, Latin America, and Asia. Twelve professional anthropologists and economists visited these

> societies and played standard ultimatum, public goods, and trust games with the locals. As in advanced industrial societies, members of all of these societies exhibited a considerable degree of moral motivation and a willingness to sacrifice monetary gain to achieve fairness and reciprocity, even in anonymous one-shot situations. More interesting for our purposes, we measured the degree of market exposure and cooperation in production for each society, and we found that the ones that regularly engage in market exchange with larger surrounding groups have more pronounced fairness motivations. The notion that the market economy makes people greedy, selfish, and amoral is simply fallacious.[26]

As it turns out, the strongest cultural predictor that participants will play fairly with strangers is how market-oriented their society is. People from market societies characteristically know how to put themselves in their trading partner's shoes. People from non-market societies do not.

Other studies produce similar results. Zak and Stephen Knack have shown that market societies also tend to be high-trust societies, while non-market societies tend to be low-trust societies.[27] Omar Al-Ubaydli, Daniel Houser, and colleagues have shown that "priming" people with words related to markets and trade makes them *more* (not less!) trusting, trustworthy, and fair in experiments.[28]

Institutionalist economics often argues that market exchange does not rely upon self-interest alone. It also relies upon—and at the same time tends to reinforce—mutual trust, reciprocity, and trustworthiness.[29] Market systems require a high degree of generalized trust and trustworthiness to function. Consider the fact that I could fly to Hong Kong, a city I have never visited, flash a credit card, and be supplied a luxury car, all on my promise to pay. Somehow, market societies make this promise mean something.[30]

To illustrate this further, every year the Fraser Institute, a free-market think tank, ranks countries by how free market their economies are. Their top 10 in 2012 are Hong Kong, Singapore, New Zealand, Switzerland, Australia, Canada, Bahrain, Mauritius, Finland, and Chile. Denmark is ranked #16. The United States is #18. Transparency International, an NGO focused on fighting political corruption, publishes a "Corruption Perceptions Index," which ranks how corrupt countries are perceived to be. According to Transparency International, these are the top 10 least corrupt countries: Denmark, New Zealand, Singapore, Finland, Sweden, Canada, the Netherlands, Australia, Switzerland, and Norway.

You may notice quite a bit of overlap between the most economically free and the least corrupt countries. That's not a coincidence. As Figure 3.1 shows, there is a positive correlation between countries' degree of economic freedom (as measured in by the Fraser Institute's economic freedom

Figure 3.1 Economic freedom vs. corruption

ratings) and countries' lack of corruption (as measured by Transparency International's Corruption Perceptions Index[31]).

This kind of empirical work is not the final word. It does not decisively prove that market societies foster better motivations than socialist societies. However, it is better than hypothesizing from the armchair, as philosophers are apt to do. The only way to know whether capitalism is corrupting or ennobling is to do bona fide social scientific research. The extant research strongly suggests Cohen is wrong.[32]

Cohen spent his life arguing about how community and fellow feeling are the highest values. Yet, he did little to investigate what actually helps promote them. He lived in one of the most fraternal places in history, but condemned it in favor of far less fraternal places because he could *imagine* those other places behaving better.

At this point, we can see that Cohen's argument for socialism is unsound. Cohen has failed to show us that socialism is the ideal social system. His argument rests on two serious fallacies which all philosophers must avoid. It wasn't obvious at first what his mistakes were, but now we know.

However, I do not just intend to show that Cohen's argument is fallacious. Chapter 4 explains how Cohen helps us see that capitalism is the intrinsically best system.

Why Utopia Is Capitalist

Four

I do not laugh at the content of our wishes that go not only beyond the actual and what we take to be feasible in the future, but even beyond the possible; nor do I wish to denigrate fantasy ...

—Robert Nozick, *Anarchy, State, and Utopia*

WHAT IS UTOPIA?

Imagine a world much like ours, but with one big difference: in this parallel world, everyone is morally perfect. Whatever morality requires, people do it, and do it without grumbling. In this parallel world—let's call it *utopia*—people always do the right thing for the right reason, know what they are doing, and feel the right way about it. In this world, everyone has a perfect sense of justice, and always does what justice demands.

Cohen thinks that theories of justice should involve idealizing human nature. Cohen's question is: What principles would people live by, and what institutions would they live under, if only people had perfect moral motivation? (Or, at least, it asks this if only people always were motivated to do what is morally required, if not necessarily to go above and beyond the call of duty.) For Cohen, a theory of justice and of just institutions is a theory of ideals. It is in that sense utopian. It does not involve imagining that people have

DOI: 10.4324/9781003424116-4

superpowers, that there is no bad luck, or that milk and honey flow magically in the rivers.

Some philosophers think there is no point in asking Cohen's question. They say the answer might provide us with little practical advice about what to do here and now. A world in which everyone always did the right thing is desirable, but it's also unrealistic.

Cohen would respond that utopian theorizing, so defined, has a clear point: it tells us what justice requires. A fully just society is, among other things, a society in which every person always does the morally right thing for the right reasons. A just society is a society in which everyone is committed to justice. After all, if you imagine a society in which people sometimes did wrong things, you'd be imagining a society with injustice in it, and thus be imagining a less than fully just society. So, if you want to know about what justice requires, you have to ask what rules and institutions would be best if everyone always did the right thing. (Asking what is the just response to other people's injustice is a secondary question, he thinks.)

Further, Cohen would add, justice doesn't ask more of people than they can do. Justice doesn't require that people fly like Superman or use telepathy like Wonder Woman. Justice just requires that people do things that many real people are not willing to do, because they are too cruel, callous, or selfish. In that sense, a just world is easily attainable, even if unrealistic. It only requires each of us to choose to do what's right.

At the very least, utopian political philosophy tells us something about the institutions we live under. It tells us where things stand, morally speaking. If you are at all reflective, you will wonder at times, just how bad is the world, compared to how things should be, and easily could be, if only we were willing to do what morality requires? (I'll consider this question in more depth in Chapter 6.)

It's unrealistic to expect we will ever live in a world where everyone is morally perfect. But we should not be complacent, and assume we cannot do much better than we do now. After all, 30,000 years ago, human beings lived in small, poor, diseased family clans that were in constant war with one another. In prehistoric times, the percentage of men dying in armed combat with men from other tribes might have been as high as 60%.[1] Imagine trying to tell people back then that it would be far better to live as people do in modern-day Switzerland. You'd be dismissed as silly and utopian. But we know better now—we know that we can live much better now than we used to. Can we really conclude that we cannot learn to live even better than we do now?

IS UTOPIAN CAPITALISM AN OXYMORON?

When I first read Cohen's *Why Not Socialism?*, I realized that the essential flaw was that he was not comparing like to like. I recognized that he argued for the inherent moral superiority of socialism by comparing idealized socialism to realistic capitalism, when he should have been comparing idealized socialism to idealized capitalism.

Cohen's argument involved a kind of cheating, but I doubt Cohen realized he was cheating. Cohen probably thought there was no need to compare ideal capitalism to ideal socialism, because he thinks that "ideal capitalism" is an oxymoron—you know, like "business ethics" or "military intelligence." Cohen probably assumed that if people had perfect motivations, they'd dispense with private property and the market altogether.

Many pro-capitalist philosophers and economists seem to agree. Arguments for capitalism, private property, and market economies often rely upon the idea that these institutions are a response to human failings, and that under utopian conditions, we would have no need to of them. By analogy, if people were morally flawless, we wouldn't need criminal courts or prisons.

For instance, the eighteenth-century philosopher David Hume—himself a classical liberal capitalist—argued that if people had pure motivations, there would be no need for private property.[2] Hume says that questions about justice in property arise only when there is moderate scarcity and limited fellow-feeling:

> suppose ... the mind is so enlarged, and so replete with friendship and generosity, that every man has the utmost tenderness for every man, and feels no more concern for his own interest than for that of his fellows; it seems evident, that the use of justice would, in this case, be suspended by such an extensive benevolence, nor would the divisions and barriers of property and obligation have ever been thought of ... Why raise land-marks between my neighbour's field and mine, when my heart has made no division between our interests; but shares all his joys and sorrows with the same force and vivacity as if originally my own?[3]

The idea here is that if we had no differences in interests and if we loved every other person as strongly as we love ourselves, we would have no need for private property. Since a necessary (if not sufficient) feature of capitalism is that it has private property in the means of production, no private property means no capitalism.

It's worth noting here, in passing, that Hume isn't exactly saying that if we had such altruistic motives, we would be socialist. Socialism is a system of *collective* rather than private property. Under socialism, the group asserts ownership rights to property against individuals, whereas in capitalism, individuals assert ownership rights to property against other individuals and the group. Hume, I think, is making the more radical claim that if we were perfectly altruistic, we would dispense with property notions altogether, with both capitalist private property and socialist collective property. Hume means that if we were perfectly generous and altruistic, we would have *no* ownership, which is not quite the same thing as socialist ownership.

More recently, Schmidtz argued, in his "The Institution of Property,"[4] that private property is justified in order to ensure that people maintain rather than destroy resources. Private property prevents what ecologist Garrett Hardin calls the "tragedy of the commons." The "tragedy of the commons" refers to the tendency for unowned resources—resources that everyone is free to use—to be overused and destroyed. For example, since no one owns the fish in the oceans, people try to snatch as many fish as they can before others do. But then fishing stock starts to disappear. Schmidtz says this creates an imperative: if we want to leave enough and as good for others, if we want our children to inherit a world full of resources, we often *must* remove resources from the commons. If we leave things in the commons, the resources will be destroyed. At the same time, because privatized resources can and will be used more productively, privatization *increases* the stock of what can be owned, even if it decreases the stock of what can be appropriated. So, for instance, the typical American today is something like twenty times richer than the early settlers of the United States.

Schmidtz's argument relies upon sad and unfortunate facts about human selfishness and mutual distrust. Cohen could agree with Schmidtz that the need to avoid a tragic commons could justify private property in the real world, with real people, but Cohen would deny that this tells us anything about what justice requires. Justice, Cohen says, is what happens when people are so well motivated that they would not cause a tragic commons.

And so, Cohen concludes, again, that private property and markets are merely useful social technology in light of human vice. Sure, his argument in *Why Not Socialism?* compares ideal socialism to realistic capitalism. When I claim he should have compared ideal socialism to ideal capitalism, Cohen would probably respond that there's no such thing as "ideal capitalism."

For a while, I wondered if this response was right. It was hard to visualize what ideal capitalism would be, a capitalism that would serve as a counterpart to Cohen's ideal socialist camping trip. But that changed upon watching the *Mickey Mouse Clubhouse* television show with my younger son. I noticed that *Mickey Mouse Clubhouse* presented the capitalist ideal: a voluntaryist, anarchist, non-violent, respectful, loving, cooperative society.

PROPERTY RIGHTS: A BRIEF DESCRIPTION

The distinctive features of capitalism are (A) extensive private property (including groups of private citizens), especially in productive capital goods or the "means of production," (B) voluntary trading of private property on the market, and

(C) that every person possesses an extensive sphere of *individual* economic liberty in which she has may make decisions as she pleases for herself. Before moving on to explain why A–C would be valuable even in utopian conditions, I need to explain briefly just what private property is.

When we say that Minnie Mouse *owns* the Bowtique, or that she *has private property rights* in her Bowtique, we mean that:

1. Minnie may use the Bowtique at will. That is, under normal circumstances, she can feel free to use it when she pleases, how she pleases, provided she respects others' rights.
2. Minnie may alter or even destroy the Bowtique.
3. Minnie may sell, give away, rent, or otherwise transfer the Bowtique to others.
4. She may use the Bowtique to earn income.
5. Minnie may exclude others from using, changing, destroying, or interacting with the Bowtique. Others may not use the Bowtique without Minnie's permission.
6. If others harm or destroy Minnie's Bowtique, they owe her compensation.
7. Other people have a moral obligation to respect 1–6; they are morally obligated not to interfere with Minnie as she uses, modifies, transfers, excludes, or destroys the Bowtique.[5]

So, a private property right is not really one unified right, but a bundle of related rights. Together, these rights give the owner a wide degree of control and discretion over an object, and at the same time, exclude other people from exerting control over that object.

Note that when we say that Minnie may use the Bowtique at will, we don't mean that she may do just anything she wants with it. Our rights are always limited by other people's rights. Consider: I have a right to free speech, but that right doesn't imply that I am free to show up in your bedroom at 2 a.m. to recite the lyrics of "Raining Blood." Similarly, Minnie has the right to use her bow-making equipment as she sees fit within a wide range of possible uses, but that doesn't mean she can use it to murder other people. I have a right to own a guitar, but not the right to smash you in the face with it. Exactly how all of our rights fit together is a complicated philosophical question. I won't expand on the point here, since there's no special problem here for property rights as opposed to rights in general, and since the question of how rights fit together is reasonably well understood.

Note also that property rights need not be considered absolute. They might instead be what philosophers call *prima facie* rights. The difference between absolute and *prima facie* rights concerns whether other moral considerations can ever trump or override these rights. Absolute rights can never be trumped or overridden. But *prima facie* rights can be. So, for instance, my property right in my lawn forbids you from running on my lawn without my permission. You may not just choose to run around on my lawn because you would enjoy doing so. However, suppose you were being chased by ravenous zombies and needed to cross my lawn to get away. If my property rights were absolute, it would be wrong for you to run across my law as you flee. However, if property rights are *prima facie* rights rather than absolute rights, then you may run across my lawn to get away. For reasons like this, philosophers tend to think property rights are prime facie rather than absolute.

Note also that while ownership is a bundle of rights, we can own different things in different ways. Sometimes we own things, but this ownership doesn't include all the particular rights listed above. For instance, Mickey owns a real dog, Pluto, while Donald owns a stuffed toy lion, Sparky. The way Mickey owns Pluto is different from how Donald owns Sparky. Donald may destroy Sparky at will, or slice Sparky up, or give Sparky to a person he knows will abuse the toy. But Mickey cannot do any of those things with Pluto, even though he owns Pluto. And so it goes with other things. Sometimes we own houses that come with restricted covenants, or pool club memberships we can sell only in confined ways. How we own things varies from thing to thing.

So that's what private property amounts to. Why would the saintly Mickey Mouse Club villagers want any of it?

PRIVATE PROPERTY IN UTOPIA

The Clubhouse Villagers are close enough to morally perfect (and their society was small enough) that they could dispense entirely with private property. Many of the instrumental justifications for markets and private property do not apply to them. Nevertheless, even though the villagers are even more virtuous than Cohen's socialist campers, the villagers have private property in the means of production. They have privately owned stores, farms, factories. And, in watching the show, I saw that it makes sense that they would have private property and markets, even if, strictly speaking, they don't *need* to do so. It's not that the villagers *must* be capitalist—in their utopian conditions, they are not required to be capitalist. As I will explain below, it would be fine for them each to choose to form or join a socialist commune instead. Rather, the point is that they *can* be capitalist, and they get *value* from doing so. Private property makes their lives *better*.

The best way to see that it makes sense is just to watch the show, and see if you have any moral complaint against their capitalist activities. You'll be hard pressed—as my description of their capitalist behavior in Chapter 2 was apt. As it turns out, any moral flaws that exist on the show are incidental—they exist only for branding purposes, humor, to create drama, or to teach toddlers moral lessons.

The philosopher Loren Lomasky points out that people (and by extension people-like mice, ducks, and giants) are project-pursuers. They have ideas and visions that they want to implement. Pursuing projects over the long-term is often part (if not the only part) of what gives coherence and meaning to our lives.[6] To express ourselves, develop ourselves, craft ourselves, and so on, often requires that we have sustained and exclusive control of objects over time. And so most people have an interest in controlling certain objects over time.

If Minnie owns a bow factory, this means she may use it at will as she sees fit, but other people may not use it (modify it, destroy it, move it, etc.) without her permission. Minnie has a particular vision or set of goals she wants to achieve. She has projects she wants to engage in. To do so, she needs *stuff*, and she needs to be able to count on using that stuff in a sustained way over time. If the materials of the Bowtique were up for grabs—if anyone could just use them, even on a set schedule—she would not be able to pursue her vision of the good life. She needs the Bowtique to be *at her disposal*. The Bowtique is her creation, her vision, her project. Even though Minnie is happy to work with others on many other projects, it means something to her to control the Bowtique alone. She can count on being able to run her Bowtique as she pleases. Minnie takes a certain pride in having a bow factory that is hers, not because she's fetishistic about consumption or control, but because this gives her an avenue to exercise her talents and achieve excellence in a long-standing project.

Similar remarks apply to the other characters. Willie the Giant wants to farm. In an imaginary ideal socialist economy, the nice socialists would no doubt let Willie plow the collectively owned fields with the collectively owned plow. But that's not good enough. Willie wants a farm that he can shape according to his vision. He wants the farm to be *his*, not because he's selfish and mean, but because he wants to realize his own personal plans and ideas of how farming should go. For that to happen, he needs to have property that he can use at will and that others will refrain from using.

It's not just that Minnie, Donald, and Willie want exclusive use-rights over objects. They also want to be able to use, give away, sell, and in some cases destroy these objects, as part of their pursuit of their visions of the good life. It means something for Minnie to be able to sell Bows to others—that others are willing to buy from her *because they like the bows* rather than as a favor to her. It means something to Clarabelle that she can choose to sell her muffins or instead give them to a sick friend. And so on.

Some philosophers—themselves having never owned a business or a farm—might have a hard time understanding these kinds of desires. But if that philosopher can understand why one might want to write a book by oneself, rather than with co-authors or by committee, the philosopher can similarly understand why someone might want to own a factory or a farm or a store. Or, if an artist can understand why one might want to paint by oneself, rather than having each brushstroke decided by committee, or rather than having to produce each painting collectively, then the artist can similarly understand why someone might want to own a factory or a farm or a store.

Another closely related reason for having private property, even in utopia, has to do with the sheer aggravation of always having to ask permission. Imagine everything belonged to everybody. Now imagine every person loves each other very much. Still, every time you go to use something, you'd have to check and see if anyone else needed or wanted to use it. ("Hey, does anyone need the laptop right now?") Or, otherwise, we'd have to develop conventions such that you knew, without asking permission, that you could use things at certain times. ("Oh, good, it's 6 p.m. My turn to use one of the village laptops.") There's something deeply annoying about that, even if we love others as much as we love ourselves. We want to have a range of objects that we can count on to be free to use *at will*, without first having to ask permission or to check with others or to follow a schedule. Without the right to make use of a range of objects at will, we will feel stifled and repressed.

People have a need to feel "at home" in the world. Most of us are at home in our homes because we may unilaterally shape our homes to reflect our preferences. Our homes are governed by principles we endorse. We do not have to deliberate in public and justify our furniture arrangements to others in society. To the extent that we have private property, we acquire the means to carve out a space for ourselves in which we can be at home. That's not to say that we cannot also feel at home in a collective. Mickey and Minnie enjoy communal activities and property just as much as they enjoy private activities and property. The important point is that most of us need both—we need at times to participate in a larger community, and we need at times to escape to our private ventures and spaces. Without private property, we cannot do the latter.

Note further that, in pursuing our projects, it's not just that sometimes I need access to an electric guitar or that Michelangelo needs access to paint. Rather, there's an additional value to be gained from having access to the same electric guitar and the same paintbrushes over time. Over time, we incorporate objects in the world into our lives—they form part of our histories.

Consider any object to which you have a sentimental attachment, such as china dolls you inherited from nana, or the guitar you purchased after you got your first book contract. Would you be indifferent if a genie told you that, while you were sleeping, he destroyed the object, but then replaced it with a chemically and structurally identical object? Or would you think something is lost?

Note that the same can be said about the people we love. As Robert Nozick once noted, we don't usually just "trade up" as soon as we find willing partners who are, all things considered, higher quality than our current partners.[7] One major reason why is that we *incorporate* those we love into our identities, or we incorporate ourselves into a "we" with that person. Our histories get bound up together. If a genie killed my wife tomorrow but instantly replaced her with a doppelganger (with the same physical composition, memories, and such), I might well decide to go on living with the replacement (especially for the kids' sake), but I'd still feel alienation and grief.

We form relationships with some objects, with some of the things we own, with the books we write, with the artwork our children make us, and so on. This is not just a toy cheetah, but the very toy cheetah we joked like to eat monsters at night and so would keep my son safe from harm as he slept. This is not just a hammer, but the hammer my uncle used when he built his own house after the war. This is not just a Mustang, but the Mustang Steve McQueen drove in *Bullitt*. And so on. And this is yet another reason why the Clubhouse Villagers have private property, even though they are so generous and kind that they could make do without it. They form relationships with particular objects and incorporate those objects into their lives.

Socialists might object that if the other villagers know that Minnie is so attached to the bow-making equipment, they might, out of love and generosity, just let her use it all the time, allow her to give it away and sell it, etc., though they would insist that in some sense the bow-making equipment belongs to all, not just Minnie. I'm not sure this qualifies as an objection, though. Instead, I see it as saying that socialists would recognize that there are good reasons, even in utopia, to give people exclusive control of certain objects—that is, to give people property rights.

There is another reason for private property, when we try to practice utopia on a grand scale: the limits of our knowledge. We have imperfect information. Sure, in a small village, we might all know that the nice thing to do is let Minnie use the Bow-making equipment whenever she wants. And so maybe there'd be little harm in saying that the equipment belongs to all, but we'll just all choose to let Minnie possess it "as if" she had property rights in it. But in a large society, there's just no way to scale this kind of thing up. I don't know enough about other people, what their needs and desires are, or how different objects fit into their plans or projects.

Related to this point: In previous work, Schmidtz and I have argued that private property is useful to help us form expectations:

> Consider, then, the point of property rights. In a way, such rights are like fences: their whole point is to *get in the way*. Or, if putting up fences does not sound liberating, consider a different metaphor: rights are like traffic lights. Traffic lights facilitate movement not so much by turning green as by turning red. Without traffic lights, we would all have, in effect, a green light, and the result would be gridlock. By contrast, a system where we face, in turn, red and green lights helps to keep us moving. The system constrains us, but we all gain in terms of our ability to get where we want to go; for we develop mutual expectations that enable us to do so uneventfully. Red lights can be frustrating, but the game they create for us is a positive-sum one. We all reach our destination more quickly, more safely, and more predictably, because we know what to expect from each other.[8]

This is another instrumental defense of private property. But notice that this defense does not essentially rely upon the idea that private property is necessary to rescue us from problems arising from our *moral* failings. Here again the issue is cognitive, not moral.

Adding to this, and staying with the traffic metaphor, consider the rules we use for four-way stops:

1. Whoever arrives first, gets to go first.
2. In the case of simultaneous arrival, whoever is on the right goes first.

3. If literally all four people arrive at the same time, resolve the conflict by waving.

We also have a rule for emergencies:

4. Let the person with a known emergency go first!

The fourth rule distributes the right of way according to need, while the other three do not. If the fourth rule—the need-based rule—trumps the others, why not just replace rules 1–4 with a new rule:

5. At any four-way stop, whoever has the most need gets to go first.

In fact, there's an obvious reason why not. Imagine what it would be like to live like that. We'd have to stop, get out of our cars, and have a conversation each time we come to a four-way stop. Even if we were all perfectly honest and good, this kind of rule would just be too costly. Distributing according to need is not what we need.[9] This is not because we are morally flawed, but because we have cognitive limitations.

Some socialists (though not, I think, Cohen) would object here that they have no problem with people owning *personal*, non-productive property, like toothbrushes or guitars they use in hobbies. They only have a problem with people owning productive property, like farm equipment or bow factories. But there are two big problems with this.

First, it's not clear there's a deep distinction between productive and non-productive property. John Petrucci's signature Music Man JP6 guitar is productive property he uses to earn a living; my Music Man JP6 guitar is non-productive property I use for fun. Eddie Van Halen uses his EVH 5150 III amplifier to earn a living; I use one for fun. Does this mean, from a socialist perspective, that it's bad to let Petrucci have his guitars or Van Halen to own his amps, but fine for me to have them? Similarly, is it wrong for Hertz to rent cars to make money, but okay for you to own those exact same cars to drive yourself to work or your kids to soccer practice? Is it okay for Scrooge McDuck (in his *DuckTales* incarnation) to have his massive pile of money, so long as he uses it just for swimming and not as capital for investing? Is it okay for my aunt Jackie to own a loom as a decoration, but does it become wrong if she then starts making and selling fabric with it? For the most part, it seems like the difference between productive and non-productive property is just how we use it. So, at most, socialists don't really oppose allowing people to own private "productive property"; they oppose allowing people to use their private property in a productive way.

Second, it's not clear why, in *ideal* conditions, socialists would have any problem with people owning productive property. Socialists—such as many of the Occupy Wall Street protestors—object that allowing private ownership in the means of production leads to all sorts of problems—such as exploitation, treating people as instruments, objectionable inequality, a lack of opportunity, or whatnot—but these problems occur only under real-world conditions, not in utopian conditions. In the utopian conditions of Clubhouse capitalism, capitalist factory owner Minnie Mouse would never exploit anyone, because she is too nice. Capitalist Minnie Mouse would never allow objectionable inequalities or a lack of opportunity, because she and others like her would just choose to give the deserving poor what they need. And so on. Socialists' moral objections to private property apply only in non-ideal, non-utopian conditions. They are *irrelevant* in this debate. In our world, we might all agree that Occupy Wall Street has some legitimate complaints, even if we do not all agree on their proposed solutions. But there is no Occupy (Main Street, USA?) movement in the *Mickey Mouse Clubhouse* world, because none of the occupiers' complaints apply to ideal capitalism.

So, to summarize, there is a range of reasons to have private property, even in utopian conditions. People get value from having objects that they can use at will, without having to ask permission from others. They get value from being able to pursue projects, and to do so, they sometimes need objects over which they gain exclusive control. People have grounds for wanting to be able to pursue projects alone, rather than doing everything collectively. They find value in having spaces that are all their own, so that they can feel "at home" in those spaces. People can form sentimental attachments to particular objects that have a special history. And, finally, the most effective way of making sure people have the objects they need for their projects is often to follow the rules of private property, rather than treating everything as if were a common pool to be distributed according to need. Sure, in utopia, we could make do without private property, but private property makes utopia better.

MARKETS AND ECONOMIC LIBERTY IN UTOPIA

We've established why, even under utopian conditions, people would get additional value from having private property. Now let's discuss further why they would get value not just in having private property, but also in buying, selling, and trading this property in markets, and in having a wide sphere of economic liberty. A capitalist society endows each person with a wide sphere of economic freedom. Why would people in utopian conditions value having such a wide sphere? Here I'll discuss two sets of reasons, one having to do with how markets help achieve prosperity, and one having to do with the goal of having people be the authors of their own lives.

First, markets are important to ensure that people can be as prosperous as possible. Even in utopian conditions, market societies will outperform socialist societies in economic terms. Some socialists might balk here that we should not be so focused on filthy lucre. But Cohen, I think, would disagree. Marxists say that real liberty is not just the absence of interference from others, but also the effective power, capacity, or ability to do what one wills. Call this conception of liberty *positive liberty*. For example, a bird has the positive liberty to fly, but human beings do not. Cohen once argued that "to have money is to have freedom."[10] He says that money, or more precisely the real wealth that money represents, is like a ticket that gives people access to the world. The more wealth one has, the more one is able to do, and in that sense, the more freedom one has. If we care about people having positive liberty, then we care about making them as wealthy as we can. As the former paramount leader of communist China Deng Xiaoping is thought to have said, "To get rich is glorious!" I agree. In my ideal world, everyone who wants to be is a googolplexinaire.

Now, keep in mind that trade is usually—and especially in utopian conditions—a positive-sum game. That is, when people are free to make trades and free to walk away from any trades they don't want to make, then such trades will usually benefit both parties. In a market exchange—even in real-world capitalism—both parties to the trade make a profit. The difference between utopian and real-world capitalistic trading has to do with motivations. In the real world, we are fairly selfish, and so are less concerned with how well our trading partners do. In utopian capitalism, we are more strongly motivated to make sure the other party to the trade does well.

In a class I teach on political economy, I illustrate the concept of gains from trade by doing an in-class experiment. As students enter, I give each of them a different candy bar. I ask them to rate the candy they received on a scale of 1–10, with 1 meaning they hate and 10 meaning they love the candy. I then add up their scores. (For instance, in a fall 2013 seminar with 19 students, the total was 103.) After, I tell them they are free to make trades with any willing partner they wish. Most students make a trade, and everyone who trades is happier with her new candy than she was with the old. After all trading is ceased, I ask them to rate the candy they now have. Usually, the total value of the candy goes up 30–50%. (For instance, in the fall 2013 seminar, the final total was 149.) I then ask students, is there some way we could have made it possible to have even higher gains from trade? Usually they conclude that if we had even *more* students trading a greater variety of candy bars (or even things other than candy bars), the gains would have been even higher. And so, in ten minutes, the students discover first-hand what Adam Smith explained in the first few pages of the *Wealth of Nations*: the greater the size of the market, the greater the potential prosperity we can all enjoy.

Economists have long understood that in a market economy, the systematic effect of private citizens' pursuit of private ends is to create background conditions of wealth, opportunity, and cultural progress. Each of us does as well as we do because of the positive externalities created by an extended system of social cooperation. This extended system of cooperation explains why each of us in contemporary liberal societies have our high standards of living and easy access to culture, education, and social opportunities. We are engaged in networks of mutual benefit, and we benefit from other people being engaged in these networks. When we go to work in business, we help create, sustain, and improve these networks of mutual benefit. When things are going well—and overall they tend to go well—we create a series of positive externalities through our innovations, through the division of labor, and by helping to create economies of scale.

This is all true of real-world markets. Would it be less true of markets in utopia, if utopia even has such markets? Keep in mind that in utopia, by definition, people are too nice to cause certain problems that occur in real-world markets. In utopian capitalism, you don't have to worry about deception or "information asymmetries"—the mechanic never charges you for unnecessary work, and the used car salesperson always tells you the whole truth about the car. In utopian capitalism, you wouldn't have to worry about exploitation—the buyer wouldn't dare take advantage of your bad luck in order to offer you a low price. In utopia, no one tries to corner the market through monopolies or monopsonies. In utopia, everyone gladly contributes his or her fair share to public goods, knowing full well that everyone else will too.

Recall from Chapter 1 that all economic systems need information, incentives, and learning. By "information," I mean that people need some signal that tells them how to coordinate their actions with others. By "incentives," I mean that people need something that induces them to act on that information. And by "learning," I mean that, since in the real world people respond imperfectly to information and incentives, we need something that trains people to respond better. In real-world conditions, socialism faces an incentive problem.

In utopian conditions, socialism's incentive problem disappears. However, the information problem remains. Thus, under utopian conditions, if people want to benefit from having a large-scale division of labor and being able to cooperate and work together with hundreds of thousands, millions, or billions of others, they will need to use markets.

In real-world capitalism, we often make trades with people for whom we have only minor, diffuse concern. In utopia, though, everyone is motivated by a strong desire to promote the common good and the good of all. But this is a reason to use markets, not a reason to avoid them. In an ideal society, everyone is supposed to be motivated to promote the good of all, not just her own good. But, if so, then most people will be strongly motivated to participate in markets. If they want to coordinate their mutual activities to promote everyone's good as best they can, the most effective way is through trade on the market. Market prices convey information about the relative scarcity of goods in light of the effective demand for those goods. Market prices thus tell producers and consumers how to adjust their behavior to scarcity and demand. When it comes to making maximal use of the information needed to run a large economy, nothing beats the market.

To illustrate this, imagine that Mickey Mouse could have a magic wand that would make everyone 30 times richer over a period of 200 years. Mickey, being benevolent, would of course wave the wand.

Now, suppose instead that Mickey Mouse could come up with an ideal economic plan, as old-fashioned socialists wanted. Imagine Mickey Mouse is some kind of noble philosopher-king (or philosopher central-planner). He determines a way for us to work together, to divide up tasks, to cooperate, and so on, such that if we follow his plan, then over the next 200 years, we will all become 30 times richer. In utopian conditions, people would *want* to go along with Mickey's plan voluntarily, because they would see that by going along with the plan, they promote the good of all. In utopian conditions, people would want to come together under Mickey's guidance to produce such wonderful outcomes. (I'm sure Mickey would as best he can make provisions for ensuring that people get jobs and tasks that they enjoy, so that they all have good lives as they go along with his plan.) When everyone follows Mickey's advice, it is kind of like waiving the magic wand.

The problem, of course, is that we don't have any such magic wand, and Mickey Mouse just isn't smart enough to come up with a functionally equivalent economic plan. Mickey is God-like in his moral character, but not in his brainpower. But the good news is that mainstream economics tells us that the market economy is, fundamentally, the same as the philosopher-king Mickey or the magic wand.[11] While Mickey would have offered suggestions as part of his plan, the market instead offers prices, profits, and losses. And so, just as publicly spirited, benevolent people would want to go along with philosopher-king Mickey's plan, they would want to participate in the market and respond to the signals the market sends. To follow the price signals of the market would be to serve the common good of each and all.

That's not to say that everything in capitalist utopia will be done via for-profit business. Capitalist utopia would probably have a robust civil society, full of not-for-profit institutions and communal spaces, just as we see in the Mickey Mouse Clubhouse Village. But it can benefit from having for-profit businesses too. In fact, for large utopias of thousands of people or more, markets become imperative. Mickey Mouse and Donald Duck can practice pure socialism on a small scale. Though they are nice enough to make it work on a large scale, they aren't *smart* enough to make it work on a large scale.

So, one reason to have markets in utopia is to ensure that people are prosperous and enjoy extensive positive liberty. But there is another reason as well. John Tomasi argues that people have an interest in being "self-authors," that is, in choosing a conception of the good life and finding the means to achieve that conception. For most people, if not all, this means they need a wide sphere of liberty in which to make decisions in the economic realm. As Tomasi says, people are defined by the choices they make, by what they choose to do and on what terms they choose to do it. Consider the following questions: Where should I work, and on what terms? How much should I consume, and how much should I save? *How* should I save? What should I consume? How will I decide among different possible goods and services? Is it more important to have a sports car or to take a family vacation? Should we add an addition to our house or send the children to camp for the summer? And so on. In a capitalist society, everyone is an economic planner. Everyone faces a constant stream of economic choices. How people respond to these choices both reflects and helps to determine just who they are as individuals.

Tomasi says:

> These are not mere details within a person's life. The particular pattern of decisions one makes in response to these questions about working often goes a long way to defining what makes one person's life distinct from the lives of other people. A society that denied individuals the right to make decisions regarding those aspects of their working experience would truncate the ability of those people to be responsible authors of their own lives. Indeed, denied these fuller freedoms ..., citizens would no longer *be* authors of their own lives. Decisions about matters that affect them intimately would have been taken out of their hands and decided for them by others.[12]

Many on the left have a difficult time understanding why economic decisions could have such importance when it comes to people being responsible authors of their own lives. But, Tomasi says, these same people understand easily how our decisions about social, civil, and personal matters—about whom we will love, what god we will worship and how, whom we will associate with and on what terms, what hobbies we will pursue and to what degree, what books we will read and when, what music we will listen to and how loudly, what we will choose to learn and what we will ignore, and so on—shape who we are. Most people on the left agree that if we want to allow people to be authors of their own lives, we need to grant them a wide sphere of liberty on these matters. Tomasi just says that if one can understand why it might be important to decide for oneself what and how much to read, one can similarly understand why it might be important to decide for oneself what and how much to save, invest, consume, and so on.

Now, many on the left want to reduce the sphere of economic liberty in the real world because they believe that granting people such an extensive sphere will lead to bad results. They worry that capitalists will exploit workers, that the rich will subvert democracy, that the poor will fall behind, or that the poor are too unconscientious to make rational decisions about how to spend and save. They are right, to some extent. But none of these worries apply to utopian capitalism. If we are playing by Cohen's rules, if we are talking about what a just society would look like, then we are talking about a world where people are too good and just to do anything of these bad things.

Much more can be said about why the villagers of the Mickey Mouse Clubhouse Village would remain capitalist even though they are good-hearted enough to make socialism work. However, my main argument against Cohen is this, an argument of the style he prefers: If you had to choose between living in a society much like the Mickey Mouse Clubhouse Village (but, if you prefer, with human beings rather than anthropomorphic mice, ducks, dogs, and cows) or in a society like Cohen's camping trip, which would you choose?

NOT JUST UTOPIA, BUT A FRAMEWORK FOR UTOPIAS

So, which would you choose? Actually, that's a trick question. The capitalist Mickey Mouse Clubhouse Village wouldn't make you choose. And that's one of the reasons why it's morally superior.

The Mickey Mouse Clubhouse Village has a voluntarist, anarchist, capitalist, libertarian structure. While it has some collective property, it is not a commune as a whole. Yet the Clubhouse Village would *allow* a commune within its borders. If, say, the Smurfs wanted to form a commune within the greater village, the other villagers would have no problem with that.

Capitalism is tolerant. Want to have a worker-controlled firm? Go for it. Want to start a kibbutz or commune in which everything is collectively owned? No problem. The Mickey Mouse Clubhouse villagers would allow Cohen to have his permanent socialist camping trip, so long as Cohen likewise lets Minnie Mouse have her Bowtique.

There is an essential asymmetry in the capitalist and the socialist visions of utopia. Capitalists allow socialism, but socialists forbid capitalism. Capitalism permits people to own property individually, but it also permits them to own it collectively. In contrast, socialism forbids people from owning property individually, and only allows them to own it collectively. A capitalist utopia would allow people to form communes, but a socialist utopia would forbid Minnie from owning a factory by herself.

Cohen thinks it's best if everyone lives the socialist camping trip lifestyle. He would recruit everyone into the camping trip. He would, if he could, wave a magic wand that would make us all committed to communal life. He has one vision for utopia.

It's a fine vision, really, but there are other fine visions as well. The capitalist vision of utopia is bigger and broader than Cohen's. The Mickey Mouse Clubhouse Village is a libertarian, laissez-faire, market-society utopia, but allows non-libertarian, socialist utopias within its borders, so long as the inhabitants of these socialist utopias are there by choice rather than force. Capitalist utopia can contain socialist utopias within it.

As Nozick argues in his book *Anarchy, State, and Utopia*, capitalist utopia is not really one utopia, but many. It provides a "framework" in which many different utopias could co-exist in peace and mutual respect.[13] This is crucial, because

> people are different. They differ in temperament, interests, intellectual ability, spiritual quests, and the kind of life they wish to lead. They diverge in values and they have different weightings for the values they share. ... There is no reason to think that there is *one* community which will serve as an ideal for all people and much reason think that there is not.[14]

Nozick goes on: Consider all the people you know or know about. Think about, say, G. A. Cohen, Jason Brennan, Anne Hathaway, Tom Brady, Oprah Winfrey, Machiavelli, Steve Jobs, Lebron James, Virginia Woolf, Taylor Swift, Milton Friedman, Mr. Beast, Joseph Smith, Neil Armstrong, Plato, Maria Montessori, Amy Schumer, Abraham Lincoln, Lady Gaga, Norman Borlaug, Steve Levitt, Emily Dickinson, Andrea Dworkin, Ralph Waldo Emerson, Paul McCartney, John Maynard Keynes, Andy Warhol, Jillian Michaels, Deng Xiaoping, Joe Biden, Henry David Thoreau, Jean-Jacques Rousseau, Gustave Flaubert, Leo Tolstoy, Marie Curie, Kim Kardashian, Les Paul, John Muir, Elizabeth II, Rick Harrison, Mark Zuckerberg, Jimmie Johnson, Larry the Cable Guy, Nikola Tesla, Lech Walesa, Sid Vicious, Michael Sandel, Jesus of Nazareth, Enzo Ferrari, Abu al-Qasim Muhammed, John Wayne, Rodrigo Borgia, the first person you ever kissed, your neighbors, your second-grade teacher, the person who sat next to you on your last flight overseas, your parents, and you. Nozick would ask, "Is there really *one* kind of life that is best for each of these people?"[15] It doesn't seem possible to describe just *one* type of society that would serve as an ideal or utopia for each of them. This is not because we are morally flawed. It is just because we are different.

My utopia enjoys the diverse dining scene of DC and Northern Virginia. It has daily concerts by Metallica, Opeth, and Dream Theater, and wide-open roads for us to race our sports cars. Your utopia might be a quiet fishing village in Alaska. Yours might not have any sports cars—maybe everyone bikes everywhere. My utopia has sci-fi technology. Yours might eschew technology for the simple life. Cohen's personal utopia, I suppose, is a kibbutz, or maybe it's an elite university where rich communists leading capitalist lifestyles spend time chatting about how awesome kibbutzim are, all while refusing to donate their (in their own minds) unjustly acquired wealth to charity.

The Mickey Mouse Clubhouse Village would allow you to start different communities with different rules and norms. So long as the people there live there by choice, not by force, there is no problem. And, so, the Mickey Mouse Clubhouse capitalist utopia would allow a tight-knit Christian farming community here, next to a secular commune there, next to a Silicon Valley computer firm, next to So-Cal shopping mall, next to a society of hunter-gatherers, right next to something like San Francisco's Castro District.

Nozick notes that utopian writers have, with few exceptions, been so convinced of the beauty of their vision, that they have described utopia as being just one kind of community. But, Nozick says, it's more plausible that utopia is not all one thing. Instead, utopia is a collection of utopias, many different kinds of communities with many different kinds of people.

The Mickey Mouse Clubhouse Village could be not just a utopia, but a meta-utopia in which you may choose the utopia that's best for you. The capitalist Mickey Mouse Clubhouse Village is utopia not simply because it offers a beautiful vision of its own, but also because it allows other utopias to flourish within its borders. It leaves everyone free to create or inhabit the utopia of her choice with others who also choose to live there. It offers a framework in which inhabitants of one utopia can take joy in co-existing and contemplating the lifestyles of the inhabitants of other utopias.[16] The capitalist Mickey Mouse Clubhouse gives you everything Cohen's socialist camping trip gives you, and then gives you even more. If Cohen has given us a portrait of utopia, Nozick has given us an art gallery. If Cohen's socialist utopia is the *Mona Lisa*, Nozick's capitalist utopia is the entire contents of the Louvre. The slogan of capitalist utopia might be something like, "Let a hundred flowers blossom."

CONCLUSION

Cohen says our theories of justice should be about what's best period, not about what's best given how selfish and nasty people are. Justice is the thing that happens in a world where people have morally perfect motivations and always do whatever morality requires of them. In that kind of world, the problems of real-life socialism disappear. And so, Cohen claims, socialism becomes a desirable way to live. He's right.

But in that kind of world, the problems of real-life capitalism disappear as well, while many of its virtues remain.[17] And that makes all the difference. Socialists are forever offering us an inferior product. Ideal capitalism is better than ideal socialism, and realistic capitalism (of some sort) is better than realistic socialism.

The *Mickey Mouse Clubhouse* shows us, to our great surprise, that when we judge systems by Marxist philosophical standards, capitalism becomes the most intrinsically desirable way to live. And, surprisingly, one reason Clubhouse Capitalism becomes the most desirable way to live is that for some small percentage of us, socialism is the most desirable way to live.[18] In the real world, capitalism encourages entrepreneurs to provide you with the things you want at prices you can afford to pay. In the ideal world, capitalism does even better: it gives you the opportunity to live in your personal utopia.

Anti-Social Egalitarianism?

Five

All theories of justice give *some* role to equality. For instance, most of us agree that justice requires we treat like cases alike.

Cohen and many socialists think justice requires *material equality*. In their view, justice isn't achieved until we each have equal amounts of wealth and income, work equally hard, experience equal opportunities, and have equal personal welfare.

At the limit—that is, when egalitarians follow their premises' logical implications—egalitarianism says that privileged parents shouldn't read to their kids (because it disadvantages kids whose parents don't read to them),[1] or should not prefer attractive romantic partners (because discriminating in favor of beauty means rewarding people for undeservedly winning a genetic lottery).[2] Many egalitarians don't want to accept such conclusions, but it's unclear how they can avoid doing so in a principled way. If you think no one should have unearned advantages, then you have to say no one should have unearned advantages. It's ideologically convenient, but bad philosophy, to compartmentalize that principle to complain only about capitalist markets rather than, well, all of human life.

I described capitalist utopia as realizing five major moral principles: voluntary community, mutual respect, reciprocity, social justice, and beneficence. That's not a complete list. Since we're stipulating that people are fully good, these aren't the

DOI: 10.4324/9781003424116-5

only moral principles and ideals it realizes. Still, I refrained from saying capitalist utopia tries to realize Cohen's radically egalitarian principles of justice, which prohibit all inequalities of income and wealth, regardless of how they arise. Perhaps I could have done so—a utopian capitalist society could voluntarily equalize incomes if it wanted—but Cohen might then insist on calling the resulting market society with private ownership "market socialist" rather than "capitalist." I could in turn insist his "market socialism" is egalitarian capitalism.

Rather than enter a tiresome debate about labels, I want to explain why we shouldn't accept Cohen's material egalitarianism. Material egalitarianism at its best is beside the point and at its worst is repugnant and anti-social. Cohen barely argues for egalitarianism over his long career—he mostly calls out other egalitarians for being inconsistent or making ad hoc qualifications.

Are Cohen's original arguments for material egalitarianism any good? One way to check is to determine if his arguments or principles have perverse implications, implications which he and we are not willing to endorse. As an analogy, in *Anarchy, State, and Utopia*, Robert Nozick pointed out that left-liberals, socialists, and egalitarians make various arguments in favor of government regulation of the market, but these same arguments, as given, also imply that governments should regulate our speech, sex lives, friendships, and so on. For instance, many people say free markets are bad because they lead to inequality. They say governments should intervene in such markets and redistribute income to prevent inequality. Nozick points out that free association in friendship and romance also leads to radical inequality. Fifty years later, in 2024, numerous popular and scientific articles confirm this point. The American dating market is inegalitarian; a minority of men have options and many men are left behind. So, Nozick might ask, if inequality is a reason to regulate and redistribute, should we also have governments regulate dating or redistribute dating options? The leftist in question usually (but not always!) rejects these other implications. Nozick responds that the leftist now needs to produce a principled rather than ad hoc reason for treating the cases differently.[3] We need a principled, non-question-begging reason to think we have the right to befriend and date whomever we want, inequality be damned, but not to trade with whomever we want.

Egalitarians sometimes bite the bullet and accept the full implications of their arguments. For instance, Cohen wrote a book denying that we each own our own bodies. (He claims that the concept of self-ownership is the basis of liberalism, especially libertarianism.[4]) Cecile Fabre, one of his students, later wrote a book arguing that the state should forcibly redistribute spare eyes and kidneys.[5] (She stopped short of saying the state could require beautiful people to have sex with incels.) After all, the argument goes, we don't own our own bodies. Your body and natural endowments are (as Rawls and other egalitarians agree) nothing more than undeserved winnings (or losings) from an unfair genetic lottery. It's mere luck that I was born with two working eyes and someone else wasn't, just as it's mere luck that Rawls was born to a rich family and Nozick and I weren't.

If our eyes and kidneys are like manna from heaven, and if manna from heaven should be distributed equally, then yes, we should redistribute eyes and kidneys. A person who refuses to give up "their" spare eye isn't protecting their property in their body but hoarding valuable resources from the community. That's what egalitarianism implies, though many egalitarians are quick to deny it.

I regard these conclusions as a reductio ad absurdum of egalitarianism. But I nevertheless respect egalitarians who defend such claims. Indeed, I respect them more than the egalitarians who don't. Egalitarianism in fact has such implications, and they are at least willing to admit it and defend it rather than hide behind unmotivated ad hoc qualifications.

EGALITARIANISM AS A MISDIAGNOSIS

I worry that many arguments for material equality misdiagnose the problem and thus offer the wrong solution.

A modern left-leaning liberal or socialist might say, "Some are rich and some are poor, so we should be more equal." But, in the first instance, material equality is beside the point. The problem isn't that some people have more. it's that some people don't have enough. The poor of the third world die of starvation and disease, not inequality. Beneficence directs us to help the poor because they have too little, not because they have less.

Suppose I donate $50 to Sightsavers to cure someone of trachoma-induced blindness. Sure, I thereby make the world more equal. But equality wasn't my goal. If equality were the goal, I could instead burn the $50 and blind myself, thus reducing the gap between the worse off and me. But the moral imperative is to cure blindness, not reduce the gap. At base, the badness of blindness is the inability to see, not the inequality between those who can and can't see.[6]

Or, consider that American police often treat white people better than they treat black people. Many say this is part of "white privilege." However, even here, the problem isn't inequality per se. The problem is that they treat black people badly. We wouldn't solve the problem by training them to treat everyone just as badly. The gap is a problem, but the real problem is the bad treatment. Justice demands cops to treat everyone well (and, yes, equally well).

Or, suppose philosopher professor Mark sometimes sexually harasses female graduate students but never harasses male students. Suppose Mark realize this creates an unequal environment. If Mark started harassing male students too, this would eliminate inequality, but it wouldn't solve the deeper problem. The solution is to fire Mark.

Equality is about making people the same. Beneficence is about helping people. These are not the same thing. On its own, egalitarianism is indifferent between leveling up (helping the worst off so that they catch up with the better off) and leveling down (harming the better off so that they fall to the level of the worst off). Beneficence wants to make the badly off better off.

Cohen says he prefers leveling up to leveling down egalitarianism. He would rather everyone be equally rich than equally poor. Still, if we can't level up, he is often (maybe always) willing to level down. For instance, suppose twenty of us are at a party. There are twenty-one cookies. We each have one cookie and we each would love to eat the remaining one. Suppose we can't split it. What should we do?

One seemingly obvious solution would be to distribute the cookie by lottery. We end up unequal, sure, but we get there through fair and egalitarian means.

But Cohen thinks we should destroy the extra cookie.[7] Let me quote him:

> Imagine a peaceful anarchy ... in which manna falls from heaven and gets shared equally because the sharers think

> that's the right way to deal with manna from heaven. Now suppose an extra piece of irremovable but destructible manna falls on Jane's plot. Jane says: "I don't want this extra manna, I'm going to make a big bonfire to which you are all invited, because it's not fair for me to have more than you guys do, for no reason." ... I for one would not think Jane is being foolish. I would think she is a remarkably just person, and I think we should commend her for being one ...[8]

Cohen suggests that maybe, since Jane is so just, the rest of us should (for reasons other than justice) "reward" her (yes, that's his word) by letting her keep the extra manna, but he then says perhaps not, because that contradicts her intent, and further, she's right that it's unjust for her to have more. Justice, he says, "can be mean and spiteful, but it's still justice even then: we shouldn't confuse different virtues."[9] Justice requires equality and requires the extra manna be destroyed. Cohen is tempted, if not convinced, to say we should let her keep the extra manna, not because doing so helps her and hurts no one, but because she displayed such exemplary commitment to justice that perhaps we make a special exception for her. Still, justice requires we destroy the extra manna.

That's Cohen's view. Why believe it? Cohen often regards it as a given that egalitarianism is a baseline from which departures must be justified. In his view, it's obvious that everyone should be treated the same and have the same outcomes unless we can come up with a sufficiently good reason not to. Many less extreme egalitarians accept this basic idea. Cohen finds it easy to rip apart other egalitarians' attempts to justify departures from equality.[10]

But what if you don't already accept material egalitarianism as a baseline from which all departures must be justified? We will need a good argument from him to accept it. Later in this chapter, we'll examine his best argument for equality.

When thinking about equality and welfare, we should avoid another source of confusion. Sometimes bad situations and outcomes result from unequal treatment. For instance, blacks in the US are more than twice as likely than whites to live in poverty. White people complete college at a higher rate than blacks. Some of this results from slavery and past racism. Unequal treatment in the past can cause inequalities that persist into the future. Unequal treatment in the past causes some families to develop more human and financial capital, which in turn helps their children and grandchildren do better. But, again, we must be careful in diagnosing what the real problem is. The deeper problem here is that blacks were treated badly in the US, not that they were treated *worse* than whites. If I could go back in time to 1619 and make it so that 95% of whites in the US were also slaves, or make it so that in 1890 whites in the South were subject to the same restrictions on work, trade, and migration as blacks, I would make society more equal, but not more just. The resulting society today would likely be more equal, but not a better place to live in and nothing to celebrate. Justice requires we treat like cases alike, sure, but more importantly, it requires us to treat people justly.

When we see that people today have different outcomes because of past mistreatment, we need to be careful. Are we objecting to inequality or to mistreatment? Suppose Bob and Charlie are equally talented. Out of pure caprice, their English teacher writes a glowing recommendation letter for Bob but sabotages Charlie. As a result, Bob goes to college and Charlie doesn't. Ten years later, Bob is richer than Charlie. Here, they have unequal outcomes because of unjust actions. But the fundamental objection here is to the unjust actions—to how Charlie was mistreated. Further, Bob doesn't owe Charlie compensation for Bob's greater success (he didn't do anything wrong and it's not his fault); the teacher does.

Often what looks like a good argument for egalitarianism isn't. Sometimes, upon further inspection, egalitarianism misdiagnoses the problem.

EGALITARIANISM THROUGH BAD ANALOGIES

Egalitarians often motivate egalitarianism by relying on analogies and thought experiments which elicit egalitarian intuitions. Consider:

1. Imagine that we are explorers looking to colonize a new, uninhabited land. When we arrive, no one has a greater claim to land that anyone else. Shouldn't we divide the land equally among us?[11]
2. Imagine you and I are walking in the woods. We find an unowned apple tree with two apples. Shouldn't we each get one?[12]
3. Imagine race with a finish line. We are all competing with each other. But our lanes are unfair. Some people get to start close to the finish line while others are far. Some lanes have moving walkways, some are smooth but unmoving, while others are filled with holes, traps, and obstacles. Some racers are given artificial jetpacks while others are hobbled by artificial weights. Aren't the results of the race unfair? Isn't society like that—a race with unfair lanes?
4. Imagine that we are shipwrecked simultaneously on an uninhabited island full of resources. We each have equal amounts of money or some other fungible good everyone

wants. We decide to auction all the islands' resources to determine who gets what. The auction allows that we might end up with different things based on our different preferences, but the result is fair because we each had equal starting money. Shouldn't we divide things in the real world this way?[13]

5. Imagine that grandma bakes a cake for her 193 grandchildren. There's enough for everyone to be fed. But, due to her poor eyesight, she cuts the cake unevenly. She gives 20 grandkids giant slices, 60 kids medium slices, and the rest slices too small to sate their hunger. Isn't this unfair? Shouldn't the kids with the big slices share with the rest? Isn't the real world—where some countries are rich and others not—kind of like this?

In thought experiments like these, most readers share the intuition that justice requires equality. Egalitarians use thought experiments like this to argue that justice just is equality, or that equality is the most fundamental principle of justice. That doesn't follow.

For one, the thought experiments are designed so that nothing is at stake other than equality. The thought experiments thus prove that when nothing is at stake other than equality, then equality matters, but that's all they prove. They don't prove that equality is the most important principle of justice, that it trumps other principles, or even that it matters all that much.

Take thought experiment two. Imagine you and I are walking in the woods. We find a tree with two apples. But suppose you are starving and I am full. Now it's not so obvious that we should each get one apple. Indeed, it's more obvious you should get both. Cohen might say, ah, but this means equality was a baseline from which departures had to be justified. But that's not so obvious.

After all, suppose instead we are walking in the woods and find two apples. But here the woods belong to Farmer Frannie and she planted that tree. Here's, it's obvious we should get no apples, not one each. Equality isn't a baseline from which departures must be justified. Instead, there isn't even a presumption of equality. Neither of us has even a presumptive claim to those apples.

Or, imagine we do two psychology experiments in a lab, each with two partners. We tell the first pair they're receiving $50 as an unconditional gift. We tell them to agree to a split. From their perspective, neither has a greater claim to the money. They will likely decide to split the money evenly—though they might instead base it on need or some other factor. But suppose we have the second pair of subjects take a quiz on, say, Japanese history. We tell them the amount of prize money was determined by how many questions they got right. Here, the partners might instead think they should split the money in proportion to how many right answers they got on the quiz.

Thought experiments 1–5 are meant to be analogous to the real world. Egalitarians think the real world is like the situation described in those thought experiments. So, if we judge that things should be distributed equally in those thought experiments, we should conclude that things should be distributed equally in the real world. But this follows only if the analogies are sound.

Pace egalitarians, in the real world, we are not like shipwrecked sailors, explorers, or hikers arriving simultaneously upon unowned resources, resources to which no one has a prior claim, resources just sitting there for the taking.

Instead, we live in a world where people arrive at different times. We're more like sailors, explorers, and hikers coming upon resources already in others' pockets. Further—and most importantly—we live in a world where *extracting unowned resources from the ground* is not a large source of income or wealth, with a few special exceptions. Instead, in our world, most income and wealth comes from human capital and from *doing something* productive with resources, not just capturing or extracting resources. Most of the income and wealth in our world was made, not found. We are not like sailors coming across manna fallen from heaven; we are more like sailors coming across manna others thought up, designed, engineered, and then made. The word for a sailor who thinks they have a claim to others' manna is "pirate."

We should also reject the metaphor that society is a race. It's a lousy, anti-social, anti-community way of thinking. It's also false. In a race, one person can win only if others lose. Races are zero-sum games. But society is not generally like that. Society is a positive venture for mutual gain. You getting richer doesn't automatically mean I get poorer. You succeeding in your job doesn't mean I fail in mine. You finding love and friendship doesn't automatically mean I lose love and friendship. It's not as though there is one person handing out one set of prizes and positions. It's not as though we are all racing along one track with the same finish line. We have different values and goals. There are billions of people choosing each day to interact with billions of others, with mutual beneficial transactions and interactions. In the real world, other people's gains don't usually come at my expense; instead, the collective effect of other people's mutually beneficial interactions and gains is to make me better off, too. If society were instead a zero-sum game, like a race, society wouldn't be a game worth playing.

The race metaphor is also anti-social because it presents other people's talents as a threat. In a race, what matters isn't how fast I am in absolute terms, but whether I am faster than others. Filling a racetrack with faster competitors means I lose. If I want to win, I want everyone to be slower than I am.

In society, though, while I sometimes compete and lose to people (for a spot on the baseball team, for love, for friendship) with greater talents, I generally benefit from others having more talent than I do. Economics proves this with empirical research, but you can prove that with a simple thought experiment. Imagine I wave a magic wand which makes it so, for every activity, my current level of talent and ability stays the same, but everyone else becomes worse than I am (at everything I can currently do). After waving the wand, I am no better at plumbing, farming, hairdressing, or engineering, but now everyone else is worse than I am. I would now be the best at everything and could win every competition I enter. But waving this magic wand would be a disaster for me, not just for others. My quality of life would be much worse; indeed, life would as a result become nasty, brutish, poor, and short. We might not survive a month. So, pace the race metaphor, other people's greater talents aren't a curse but a blessing. We all need others to be better at things than we are.

What the race metaphor gets right is that we shouldn't impose unfair and artificial barriers on people as they pursue their goals. But, once again, the problem isn't (in most cases) the inequality in barriers, but the barriers, period. If racist licensing laws make it harder for Bob than Charlie to get rich, justice is served by eliminating the laws, not by subjecting

Charlie to the same lousy laws. Again, justice requires that we treat like cases alike, but more fundamentally, it requires that we treat people justly.

The grandma's pie thought experiment is supposed to be analogous to rich and poor countries. Many people believe that the reason some countries are rich and others are poor is that natural resources are unevenly distributed around the globe. The rich countries are rich because they have or had access to more and better resources than the poor countries.

This view is popular among laypeople, philosophers, and historians, but economists have refuted it. It's a dead theory. Economists have subjected the view to rigorous empirical scrutiny. Economist David Weil summarizes the vast empirical literature: "the effect of natural resources on income is weak at best."[14]

For instance, China after the 1950s was and remains poorer (in per capita income and other standard measures) than Singapore or Hong Kong, though the latter have almost *no* natural resources to speak of. The USSR remained poorer than the USA throughout the twentieth century, though the USSR had far better natural resources. North Korea remained poor while South Korea became rich, though the North started with more industrial capacity and better mineral resources. In Adam Smith's time, the Netherlands and England were richer than France, though France had far better natural resources while the Netherlands was largely composed of land reclaimed from below sea level. And so on.

Indeed, while natural resources can sometimes induce growth, they more frequently *inhibit* growth. Economists call this the "resource curse": countries with a high concentration of easily extractable natural resources frequently suffer from economic stagnation. Indeed, when a country enjoys abundant resources, this encourages governments to act in destructive ways. Government officials can extract resources for their own selfish ends, and can afford to ignore or oppress their own people. Fighting over control of the resources can lead to civil war. Or, more simply, governments might create unsustainable welfare programs, programs they can only afford so long as resource commodity prices stay high.[15]

Instead, the dominant view in economics is that the reason some countries are rich and others are poor is that rich countries have inclusive institutions (like open markets and the strong protection of private property) and poor countries don't. The rich countries always have institutions which encourage stability and growth, such as open markets, strong protection of private property, and governments characterized by the rule of law. Countries which lack such institutions are always poor. Countries which shift their institutions toward effective institutions become richer; those that shift the other way become poorer.

These are my general worries about egalitarianism. I think in general it misdiagnoses problems of social justice and that most egalitarians ground their theories on irrelevant and misleading analogies. But now let's turn specifically to Cohen. He has an original and additional argument for equality other than these.

THE BORG CAMPING TRIP

Let's imagine a new egalitarian camping trip. As in Cohen's original camping trip, goods, campers once again share services, and labor responsibilities in an equal and equitable way. Once again, campers organize things to ensure everyone has an equally good time.

However, in this new trip, people insist on full equality. They insist that nothing comes between them that might undermine their sense of fraternity and community. To that end, they forbid all differences. Like *Star Trek*'s Borg Collective, everyone is the same. There are no differences in taste, values, appearance, mannerism, talents, skills, behaviors, preferences, ideas, beliefs, ethnicity, religion, lifestyle, and dreams. After all, they reason, the more distinct they are from each other, the harder it is for them to understand or empathize with each other, and so the harder it is for them to maintain community. In this camping trip, when people look at others, they thereby look in a mirror. Since they are all identical, they are all equal. Nothing makes them feel alien from one another. They are assimilated.

In this new camping trip, imagine that, as promised, fellowship and friendship indeed prevail. Imagine that people's radical similarity ensures mutual trust and cooperation. There is no conflict. Everyone gets along perfectly because everyone is the same. Their sameness means everyone understands everyone else, cares about them as equals, and never sees anyone as weird.

I do not find a society like this inspiring. I would not regard it as an ideal to which we should aspire, or as utopia about which to daydream. Frankly, I think it's rather repugnant. Fraternity or community is one value among many. The Borg Camping Trip maximizes one value to the point that it's no longer a value, and to the point that it destroys everything else that matters.

Cohen agrees, sort of. He intends to defend some kind of liberal egalitarian socialism, not the Borg's illiberal, diversity-destroying socialism. If his principles imply that the Borg Camping Trip is best, he would regard this as a reductio of his views. However, when we examine Cohen's arguments for egalitarianism, we see that he faces a dilemma. The more strictly he insists on equality, the more his arguments require him to endorse the Borg Camping Trip. But to avoid endorsing it, he must give up his arguments for material equality, which means he can't object to the inequalities that I think the Mickey Mouse Clubhouse Village might allow.

THE PRINCIPLE OF COMMUNITY

What Cohen calls the principle of "socialist equality of opportunity" "seeks to correct for *all* unchosen disadvantages, disadvantages, that is, for which the agent cannot herself be held responsible."[16] Socialist equality of opportunity permits inequality only when that inequality results from people's (responsible) choices rather than luck. Cohen remains somewhat agnostic about whether the principle of community is specifically a principle of justice, or merely a moral ideal that a perfect socialist society would realize.[17]

Cohen claims that part of what makes socialism desirable is that it uniquely allows people to be in community with one another. But, he claims, inequalities that are too large will impede or destroy such community. It is unclear just how egalitarian the principle is supposed to be, though it is clear the principle is supposed to forbid most of the inequalities that the socialist principle of opportunity would allow.[18] It's a filter that catches what a fine filter lets through.

Cohen says that socialist equality of opportunity is not egalitarian enough. He says it allows forms of inequality which are "very problematic."[19] As Cohen explains:

> The truly problematic inequality in overall benefit, the substantial inequality that is consistent with socialist

> equality of opportunity, is inequality that reflects differences in what philosophers call *option luck*. The paradigm case of option luck is a deliberate gamble. We start out equally placed, with $100 each ... We [decide to] flip a coin on the understanding that I give you $50 if it comes up heads, and you give me $50 if it comes up tails. I end up with $150 and you end up with $50, and with no extra anything to offset that monetary shortfall.[20]

Cohen clarifies that the betters begin as equals. The bet is voluntary. He adds that loser still considers it a reasonable bet and would be willing to make such a bet again. No exploitation has occurred. Still, Cohen claims, the resulting inequality is "very" morally problematic and "repugnant."[21] Good people would not make such bets and a just society, he says, would not allow them. Or, at least, a perfectly good society wouldn't have any such bets even if they were allowed.

Cohen thus complains that socialist equality of opportunity is not egalitarian enough. It allows widespread or radical inequality provided the inequalities come about the right way, such as through option luck. Socialist equality of opportunity requires equality in starting points, but not equality in results. For Cohen, then, what he calls the principle of community is supposed to forbid and eliminate the inequalities that socialist equality of opportunity would allow; it is supposed to generate equality in results. Still, Cohen does not quite tell us just *how* egalitarian this principle of community is. Does it allow *any* inequality, and if so, how much?

In some writings, Cohen seems to advocate something close to complete egalitarianism: "Egalitarians like me think justice is *fully* served only if people's access to desirable conditions of life is equal, within the constraints of a reasonable personal prerogative ..."[22] This passage suggests that justice would require 100% perfect equality were it not constrained by personal prerogative. Cohen never quite tells us just how much reasonable personal prerogative constrains the push for perfect equality, but in his example above, he says one person being $100 richer than another is beyond the pale. If we take him literally, this suggests that the space of a "reasonable personal prerogative" is tiny, and that this reasonable personal prerogative allows very little inequality. But I don't know if that's a toy example rather than his real view.

However, elsewhere, Cohen seems to suggest that the community principle allows greater inequality. He says that we "cannot enjoy full community, you and I, if you make and keep, say, ten times as much money as I do ..."[23] Perhaps, then, Cohen might think you and I cannot enjoy full community if you make twice as much money as I do (or if you win $100 from me in a voluntary bet), but here he is at least appealing to more intuitive and widely shared notions of how inequality could undermine community.

Why should inequalities resulting from option luck threaten community? His main worry, as James Otteson summarizes it, is that a rich person and a poor person live in "virtually separate worlds."[24] As Cohen elaborates, if you make ten times as much money as I do, then "my life will then labor under challenges that you will never face, challenges that your money could help me to cope with, but do not, because you keep your money ...":

> To illustrate, I am rich ... and you are poor ... You have to ride the crowded bus every day, whereas I pass you by in my comfortable car. One day, however, I must take the bus,

> because my wife needs the car. I can reasonably complain about that to a fellow car-driver, but not to you. I can't say to you: "It's awful that I have to take the bus today." There is a lack of community between us ... And it will show itself in many others way, for we enjoy widely different powers to care for ourselves, to protect and care for offspring, to avoid danger, and so on.[25]

So, Cohen complains, if I am much better off, then you and I will lead such different lives that we will not have enough common experiences, including exposure to common challenges. Since we face different challenges and have such different experiences, we will not be able to properly empathize or sympathize with one another. We will be virtual aliens to one another, and so cannot properly be in community with one another.

Cohen later returns to the example of a lottery. Suppose you eat significantly better than the rest of us because of option luck. You won a lottery that we all freely entered. Here, "even though there is no injustice …, your luck cuts you off from our common life, and the ideal of community condemns that, and therefore also condemns the running of any such lottery."[26] Here, the problem is that you are sufficiently different from the rest of us; you fail to share sufficiently in our common experiences. Here, Cohen seems to say that even if such inequality is not unjust per se, it's still morally bad, and thus morally good people would not want it or permit it.

So, to summarize Cohen's main worry is that such inequalities create differences that in turn create disconnections that in turn undermine community. An ideal of community forbids (any? almost all?) differences in wealth.

DIFFERENCE AND COMMUNITY

Cohen believes that differences in wealth translate into different life experiences, different exposure and vulnerability to challenges, and so on, that can reduce the degree to which we form a community. If I am very rich and you are very poor, I cannot fully understand and empathize with your plight. Moreover, it seems inappropriate for me to complain about many of my problems in front of you, since things I might regard as temporary misfortune—such as having to take a crowded bus to work—might be common experience for you. So, differences in wealth can bring us apart.

James Otteson reads Cohen as making the same kind of argument. As he describes the problem:

> [A rich person and poor person might] have very different home lives, different schooling and education, different vacations and job training; they will likely not eat in the same restaurants, take their children to the same parks, shop in the same stores, read the same books, watch the same television shows, vacation in the same places. ... if they happened to ride the same bus one day, they would hardly recognize each other as fellow citizens and would scarcely have anything to talk about. Cohen concludes that they can therefore share no real community ... large inequalities in wealth ... have significant costs in community.[27]

Cohen is right that differences in wealth *can* undermine community. But there are two big problems here. First, differences in wealth can bring us apart but need not do so. Instead, it is a contingent question what such differences in fact do so. It's contingent on our past life experiences, ability to empathize, on our psychology, and so on.

It's also contingent on our *choices*. Whether, how, and how much differences in wealth undermine community appears in large part to be an empirical, social scientific question, which Cohen does not try to answer.

As a graduate student, I had little difficulty being in community with my advisors, though they made at least ten times my income. Despite these differences, we had and have much stronger community with one another than we do with many others who have identical wealth. After all, we share common life experiences, common interests, and common challenges. When I was a student, my advisors had gone through roughly the same trials I had, and now that I am a professor, my students are going through roughly the same trials I went through.

That is not to say we have perfect community. But, that said, I understand them, empathize with them, and in some ways have better community with them, despite these massive inequalities of wealth, than I do with, say, my equally high-income neighbors, or even, surprisingly, than I do with my parents.

Or, consider that I can and have formed good communities with people who share my hobbies. For instance, I have a wide range of associates and friends, some of whom make a tenth of my income, and some of whom make ten times my income, but all of whom shared a passion for guitar and are "geeks" about high-gain amplifiers. We are united by common interests, if not common income.

Similarly, I know people who attend churches in which differences in income can be dramatic—some members are poor families struggling to get buy, other members are comfortable, and yet others are wealthy businesspeople who own mansions. Still, some of these church communities are as tight-knit as Cohen's socialist camping trip seems to be. At the same time, though, these churchgoers are out of community with others.

From the armchair, it seems like these sorts of points can be multiplied endlessly. Cohen is right that differences in wealth can impede us from being in full community with one another. But we know anecdotally they need not do so. Whether they do, and how much they do, is a contingent fact, depending on what we're like, how we react to differences, and what other things we have in common.

Cohen is on shaky ground. Whether (and to what degree and under what conditions) differences in wealth undermine equality is a social scientific question, to be determined through anthropological and sociological research. Cohen relies upon and cites no research in favor of his strictly egalitarian views. He sticks to intuitive philosophical arguments and anecdotes, but he needs the social scientist's toolkit. Rather than having a solid argument, he just has a hypothesis.

Worse for him, it's unclear why this counts as a complaint about inequality rather than a complaint about people's lousy responses to inequality. Cohen says inequality makes people empathize with and understand each other less. But it does not make empathy and mutual understanding hard, let alone impossible. Asking a poor person to understand and empathize with a rich person is not like asking them to bench press the moon or asking a schizophrenic to stop hallucinating. It's asking them to understand and empathize with another person despite their differences, something people often fail to do, but which they *could do* pretty easily, if only they were willing to try. (Read *Pride and Prejudice*.) I'm not an especially empathetic person but I find it easy. Why don't the rest of you?

Cohen of course argues at length that we must never dumb down justice to accommodate common moral failings. Thus, we should ask why he takes a lack of mutual understanding and sympathy as a given fact of human nature rather than a moral failing. Why not instead say that people could empathize with each other, despite their differences? Why not say that failure to do so is blameworthy and morally defective? That people tend not to do something doesn't mean they can't, he keeps saying.

This is already a compelling reason to reject Cohen's principle of community, which is the principle he uses to argue for as strict economic equality as personal prerogative allows. But there's an even bigger problem: the mechanism that Cohen uses to explain why differences in wealth should reduce community also suggests that *other* differences should be even bigger threats to community. Therefore, those other differences ought not be allowed either.

In Cohen's story, the problem with differences in wealth is not specifically differences in *wealth*, but *differences*, period. Differences in wealth are bad, in Cohen's argument, because they (could) cause us to lead very different lives and thus not sympathize with or understand each other. Sure, they can, but so can and so do other differences. People have different personalities, tastes, goals, and worries. They have differing conceptions of the sublime, the holy, the sacred, the noble, or the good. They have different philosophies and religions. They look, speak, and act differently from one another. They have different personalities, behaviors, and schedules.

All of these differences as a matter of fact cause real people to feel less connected to others, and as a matter of fact make it harder to understand and empathize with each other. It's not as though differences in money are the only or even the largest impediment to mutual empathy and understanding. All sorts of differences can undermine or reduce the community that obtains among us.

The stronger Cohen's community principle is meant to be—that is, the more strictly it demands equality—the less room it leaves for any such differences. If the principle of community is strictly egalitarian—if it forbids you from having a measly $100 more than I have—then this principle should also forbid you from being different in almost any way that would make you and I even slightly alien to one another. The more strictly Cohen insists on equality, more his theory ends up implying that the Borg Camping Trip is the ideal. But it's not good, let alone an ideal, so his argument is wrong.

But if being in community with one another is possible despite massive differences in taste, religion, views of the good, ideas of the sublime, personality, and so on—all things that demonstrably reduce community and can render people alien to another—then it should also permit massive inequalities in wealth as well. Differences in wealth are not *more* threatening to community than these other differences.

So, Cohen has a serious problem. If we accept his causal theory of how wealth undermines community, we should presume other differences undermine community just as much. Cohen does not want to portray the Borg Camping Trip as an ideal, but the more he insists on equality in income, wealth, and welfare, the more his argument implies just that.

VICARIOUS LIVING

Community is a nice thing, but not the only nice thing, or even the best thing. Upon reflection, Cohen's argument for strict equality has implications few of us, including Cohen, would be willing to endorse. Cohen's argument, if applied consistently, leaves little room for diversity or pluralism within communities.

Liberals sometimes say that justice requires that we tolerate differences among us, though they might agree, as communitarians (and Cohen) complain, that such differences can cut us off from common life and make us strangers to one another. But there is an alternative. Instead of simply tolerating each other, we can practice what Loren Lomasky calls "*toleration as vicarious achievement*":

> If the people around you are leading diverse lives, many of which are responsive to genuine goods—albeit not the ones that provide a major thrust to the activities in your own life—then the society you share with them is better for their presence. But for that same reason, *you* are better for their presence. You can *epistemically* by being made aware of the variousness of the springs of worthwhile human action ... There are also *affective* gains to be had insofar as one is inspired, uplifted, or merely entertained by episodes from others' biographies. ... we might say there are *spiritual* gains to be had by voluntarily identifying with others whose projects differ substantially from our own. By freely taking on a valuational stake in their lives, one achieves indirect association with goods to which one has no direct practical connection, goods from which one would otherwise be altogether exiled. Free-riding on the commitments and concerns of others widens and deepens one's links that that which is worthwhile.[28]

There is a plurality of worthwhile goods, projects, and modes of living, but these cannot all be realized in or achieved by just one human life. To realize all these goods and worthwhile projects, we need pluralism (i.e., we need people to live very different lives). Such diversity *could* cut us off from one another (especially if we have defective attitudes). But it could also instead allow us to live richer lives than we otherwise might. By making ourselves and our differences public, we can live vicariously through others. As individuals, we can share in one another's experiences. As we see them lead their very different lives, we can empathize with them, and, in a sense, get inside their minds.

Despite differences in theology and values, I can see great value in the life of a Cistercian monk, value that I cannot realize in my own life directly. Rather than viewing the monks as aliens with whom I cannot form community, I can, upon seeing or reading about how they live, come to share somewhat in the goods they realize through their separate lives and projects.

This applies to differences in wealth, too. An ascetic and a bon vivant realize different goods, and they can each gain from reflecting on the others' otherwise alien form of life. Our profound differences—and thus profound inequalities—are not *repugnant* because they cut us off from one another, but can be pleasing because they allow us each to better realize all the possible forms of the good life.

Cohen seems obligated to agree. First, he relies upon this very kind of empathy to motivate us to accept his socialist ideal. After all, he argues for socialism by presenting us with a form of life—the socialist camping trip—with which his readers have at best only partial experience. But they see the value in it precisely because people can and do have the ability to see through alien perspectives and vicariously experience alien forms of life.

Second, Cohen has continually argued that we should not dumb down our moral standards to accommodate the badness of human nature. People *can* empathize with one another and come to appreciate each other's differences in the way that Lomasky describes. It takes some effort—reading literature, engaging in imaginative exercises, talking to others, watching documentaries—but they can do it. Perhaps many or even most people *will* not, but as Cohen repeatedly reminds us, "will not" does not imply "cannot."[29]

CONCLUSION

I didn't describe capitalist utopia as egalitarian, though I think there are no legitimate objections an egalitarian socialist could raise against it. Cohen describes his socialist utopia as egalitarian. We should not follow his lead.

Cohen's principle of community seems appealing at first glance. However, further reflection shows this principle has many repulsive implications. For the principle of community to support Cohen's strongly egalitarian conclusions, the principle must not only forbid inequalities of wealth, but must forbid most other differences, differences we not only have no reason to reject, but differences we have every reason to celebrate. In the end, if Cohen's principle of community is strongly egalitarian, it permits at best a stunted form of community.

Material equality is sometimes an instrument for liberating people or making them better off. It is not an end in itself. The point is to liberate people or improve their welfare.

How Demanding Is Utopian Anarchism?

Six

In Federalist no. 51, James Madison says, "If men were angels, no government would be necessary."[1] That is, imagine a world full of people who are otherwise identical to us (no stronger, smarter, or faster), but who always do what's right. We wouldn't have need to use coercion and violence to maintain order. Take criminal courts, jails, and police. These institutions exist to respond to people's moral failings. If people always choose to the right thing, we would not have crime, and so we would not need institutions or people to deal with crime.

I think Madison's claim—that angels wouldn't need a state—is true, but goes too easy on us. Yes, angels would live in the cooperative capitalist anarchism in the style of the Mickey Mouse Clubhouse Village, allowing Smurf collectives on the side if anyone wants them. But saying that makes it seem as though the principles of cooperative capitalist anarchism are extremely demanding, such that while we *could* realize them, it's sort of understandable and excusable that we don't. (By analogy, you could through extraordinary willpower avoid cursing the rest of your life, but we don't really blame you when you fall short. It's within your power but it's really damn hard.)

Cooperative anarchism doesn't require angels. It merely requires *decent* people. The fact that we have states shows that

DOI: 10.4324/9781003424116-6

a large percentage of people are not merely falling short of angelhood, but are downright awful. The problem isn't that when it comes to ethics, we're not all A+, but that too many people are Fs.

DEMANDING AND UNDEMANDING PRINCIPLES

There's an intuitive distinction between what we might call demanding and undemanding moral principles. We understand that some moral ideals or obligations ask more of us than others.

Intuitively, we say moral principles are "demanding" when they have some or all of the following features:

1. They are *constraining*. Demanding moral principles give you few options about what to do and when to do it.
2. They are *time-consuming*. Demanding moral principles take lots of time to fulfill or complete.
3. They are *costly* because they require *self-sacrifice* or *the sacrifice of other values*. You have to give up a great deal to fulfill them.

And so on. The general idea is that demanding principles and ideals constrain our personal prerogative, personal freedom, eat up our time, and take away our resources.

Now consider examples of moral and non-moral principles. My concern here isn't whether any of these are *correct*. Instead, let's categorize them as demanding or undemanding.

Demanding:

> Do for others as you would do for yourself; love your neighbor as yourself; love your enemies; donate everything you don't need to charity; love God with all your heart; be

impartial between yourself and others at all times; die for your country; run into the burning building to save the child; share everything with your neighbors; make sure everyone has an equally good time at the party; never eat chocolate or sugar.

Undemanding:

> Don't do to others what you wouldn't want done to you; don't rape your neighbor; don't murder or torture your enemies; if you can save a life at little cost or effort, do so; don't blaspheme against God; don't treat others as mere tools to your satisfaction; pay your fair share for public goods you want and use, if others do so; don't commit arson; don't take your neighbor's stuff; don't treat any of your party guests badly; don't eat 3 pints of ice cream every day.

The distinction between demanding and undemanding is a continuum rather than a sharp break. Still, notice that the undemanding principles have something in common: they leave you with lots of room to do as you please, leave you in charge of your life, and don't cost you that much. Demanding principles suck up your time, make you a continuous servant of moral ends, and cost a great deal.

ANARCHISM REQUIRES MERE DECENCY

The philosopher Peter Singer argues that morality is demanding. As a kind of classic utilitarian, he sometimes argues that best you can do is the least you should do.

Singer thinks we are obligated to donate most of our income to effective charities rather than live high while people suffer and die. If it costs $1 million to keep your elderly mother alive for six more months, you should instead save hundreds or thousands of children with that same amount, who would go on to live for many decades each. Singer comes closer to living up to this demanding view of morality than most people, including me, but he doesn't come close.

Most people instead think that donating most of your income to help the desperately poor is *supererogatory*, that is, admirable and good but above and beyond the call of duty. (They don't use the technical term "supererogatory" but they accept that view.) They might imagine "angels" (in the sense of people who are otherwise like us but are morally flawless) as being disposed to do what is supererogatory, not merely what is obligatory. Angels, being morally flawless, have no trouble complying with the most demanding moral principles or ideals.

Cohen and I both agree that angels, so defined, would have no need for a state and would instead live in a kind of cooperative anarchism. I suspect he would agree with me, though, that this makes eliminating the state seem supererogatory, or like something we should or even could do only if people were disposed always to follow extremely demanding moral principles. On the contrary, anarchism isn't all that demanding.

Consider, what does utopian anarchy require?

1. Don't defraud, cheat, steal from, exploit, initiate aggression against, act with prejudice against, or impose undue risk upon other people.
2. If you voluntarily do or would make use of certain public goods, which are needed to maintain public order or which make common life better, contribute your fair share if others (will) contribute theirs.

3. Act with basic prudence (so that you don't require rescuing from others because of your lack of basic prudence).
4. From time to time, be willing to help those who need help through no fault of their own.

   People who comply with 1–4 are not angels, but *merely decent* people. Complying with 1–4 doesn't make you a morally impressive person of amazing character. You don't get a wow or a thank you for doing 1–4.

Instead, people who fail to abide by 1–4 fail to do the moral minimum. They act wrongly or even horrifically, depending on which principle they violate and how they violate it. Consistent or deep violations of 1–4 render a person bad or evil.

I described the Mickey Mouse Clubhouse Village as realizing some more impressive moral ideals. But cooperative anarchism requires less than that. It probably only requires compliance with principles 1–4, none of which are particularly demanding. If people consistently followed 1–4, it's unclear we would need any kind of state. Let's consider each principle in turn.

Principle 1 is a principle of *non-maleficence*. It doesn't require people to be impartial between their welfare and others', to serve others constantly, or to love others as themselves. It simply requires us not to mistreat others or violate their rights.

The most complex part of the principle involves assessing what counts as undue risk. Some political philosophers think the only way to solve this problem is to create an organization that has effective power to impose an answer on everyone, using violence and threats of violence. They think decent people couldn't solve this problem any other way.

Principle 2 is also not particularly demanding. Consider an analogy to group work for a university class assignment.

Principle 2 doesn't require you do the work for everyone while everyone free rides. It merely requires you do your fair share when others also do so. If everyone were decent, you could thereby be assured they would do their fair share.

Once again, some philosophers find it mind-boggling that—even if everyone were decent and knew everyone else were decent—we could each do our fair share on a mass scale without having a violent enforcement agency first define what counts as a fair share and then threaten us with violence to ensure we do it. We'll discuss that point further below.

Principle 3 is somewhat more demanding. Recall the fable of the grasshopper and the ant. The ant works in the summer, saving for winter. The grasshopper knows winter is coming but chooses not to work. When winter comes, the grasshopper starves, and so demands food from the ant. It's an interesting question whether the ant should feed the grasshopper. But it's not interesting whether the grasshopper did something wrong. The grasshopper is indeed blameworthy. By refusing to exercise basic prudence, he shifts his burdens onto the ant, tries to make the ant feel guilty, lives off the ant's sweat while he himself got to enjoy extra leisure, reduces the ant's ability to enjoy luxuries, reduces the ant's ability to contribute to bigger common projects, and reduces the ant's ability to help those who genuinely cannot help themselves. Further, the grasshopper could have been in a position to help those who cannot help themselves through no fault of their own. By violating principle 3, the grasshopper thereby by choice makes it so he cannot discharge principle 4.[2]

Recall that Cohen thinks "interpersonal test" can help us determine whether a purported motivation justifies or excuses a behavior. The interpersonal test involves asking whether a purported justification could reasonably be uttered by any member of the community.[3] Recall the kidnapper example: We can each say, "We must pay the ransom because the kidnapper otherwise will not release the victim." Bu the kidnapper cannot argue, "You should pay me because otherwise I will not release the victim" as a *moral justification* for receiving the payment.[4]

Dan Moller claims that many demands for enforced welfare payments—or even for charity from others—also fail to meet the interpersonal test. He asks us to imagine someone making a speech to their neighbors, demanding their help. Here's a slightly modified version of that speech:

> My dear assembled citizens: I know most of us are strangers, but of late I have fallen on hard times, because rather than buying insurance, saving for a rainy day, investing in an index fund, living within my means, or doing all the other things we're supposed to do, I instead maxed out my credit cards to enjoy as much consumption as I can. Now, as a result, my savings are low, and I don't have friends or family to help. Now as you know, I've previously asked for help from you as private citizens, as a matter of charity. But unfortunately that hasn't been sufficient. Thus, I'm here now to insist that you (yes you, Emma, and you, John) owe me assistance as a matter of justice. It is a deep violation if you don't work additional hours, take fewer vacations if need be, live in a smaller house, or send your kids to a worse school, in order to help me. Failing to do so is no less an injustice than failing to pay your debts.
>
> Moreover, calling this an injustice means that it's not enough that you comply with your obligations by working on my

behalf. No, I insist that you help me to *force* your fellow citizens to assist me. It doesn't matter if these others say to you that they need the money for their own purposes, that they prefer worthier causes, or if they're just hard-hearted and don't care. To the extent you care about justice, you must help me to force these others to assist me whether they wish to or not, since that is what is owed me in light of my recent bad luck.[5]

Moller and I agree that a person who makes this speech—or who thinks this way—is rather awful. Failing to live by basic prudence is a failure to oneself, but demanding others fix it mistreats them and also, if they help the imprudent, prevents them from helping those who cannot help themselves. Insisting on using violence to force them to help is evil. A minimally decent person would never dare act this way.

Nevertheless, some philosophers consider even this too demanding. I'll consider one such objection below.

Finally, principle 4 asks us to help others from time to time. It doesn't demand we give up 50% or more of our income to others. It merely asks that if we have some extra income or wealth, where consuming that income won't much affect our own welfare, that we donate some to help others who are in need through no fault of their own. Keep in mind, we are imagining doing this in a world of minimally decent people, which means no one is poor because someone violated principles 1–3.

ORDER WITHOUT VIOLENCE

The economist Edward Stringham defines "legal centralism" as the view that the "order in the world depends on and is attributable to government law."[6] Legal centralism's defenders tend to defend it on *a priori* grounds, on the basis of thought experiments. Yet legal centralism is an *empirical* claim, not an a priori claim. It's something we can test by examining the world.

When we examine the actual world, we find (pace legal centralism) that most or at least many of the working conventions that are now codified into government law arose outside government. In common law countries, such as the United States, England, Canada, and Australia, commercial law, merchant law, property law, and tort law evolved in a polycentric legal system, often completely outside of and without any backing from governments. These rules were privately enforced, often only through reputation-based mechanisms. These rules regulated commercial activity for hundreds of years and were only later adopted by and enforced by governments. The mass of the body of law that makes Western civilization work was not, as a matter of fact, created by governments, and as a matter of fact, it "worked"—it kept order—without government intervention.[7]

Further, as Stringham shows, in the real-world, government often lacks the ability, knowledge, or incentive to create and enforce good rules that would solve our cooperation problems. Government will not and often cannot enforce them.

For example, my grocery store could try adding few extra dollars to my grocery bill. You might presume that what prevents them from cheating me in small amounts is that they know I have recourse to small claims courts, the police, and the like. That's not quite right. If the store cheats me out of $5, I could take them to small claims court, but the cost to me (in terms of court fees, the value of my time, and so on), even if I win, greatly exceeds $5. The transaction costs of winning in court exceed the value of the damages. A pessimist might conclude that, as a result, people will thus always cheat each other by small amounts. But, of course, people rarely cheat each other this way. Something *other* than government enforcement—such as genuine good will, or the value of maintaining a good reputation—is doing the trick.[8]

Let's consider principle 2 in some more depth. Principle 2 tells us to contribute our fair share to public goods we want and enjoy. By definition, a public good is a good that is (mostly) non-rivalrous and non-excludable. To say that a good is non-rivalrous means that when one person enjoys or uses it, this does not diminish another person's ability to enjoy or use it. To say a good is non-excludable means that it's not possible to provide the good for one person without providing it for others. For instance, if I create an asteroid defense system to protect myself, I thereby protect everyone else. (Note that a public good is not by definition anything a government provides or ought to provide, nor is it anything with positive externalities. For instance, governments fund museums, but museums are both rivalrous and excludable.)

Economists and others argue that private markets or private associations will underprovide public goods. Presume, for the sake of argument, that people are entirely self-interested. They want public goods—such as general military protection or asteroid prevention—to exist. But, being selfish, they want to enjoy the good without paying for it, and they also don't want to be suckered into paying for the good while others enjoy it without contributing. So, they want to free-ride themselves but also avoid enabling other free-riders. Thus, the argument goes, since everyone thinks that way, few people will contribute, and the public goods will be under-provided. In order to provide public goods, we need to instantiate a government which will force people to contribute.

But even if we accept the (unrealistic) behavioral assumptions of this argument (i.e., that people always act selfishly), there already exists nevertheless a social technology, the *dominant assurance contract,* which enables private individuals to overcome the public goods problem without government, at least in many cases.

For instance, suppose we would benefit from having a monster defense force in our neighborhood. Suppose the monster defense force would cost $100,000. But everyone, selfish as they are, wants to free ride on others. An entrepreneur comes up with a scheme: To solicit contributions, she proposes the following arrangement. If you contribute the $100 and too few others contribute to meet the $100,000 threshold, your $100 is returned with a bonus of $10. Thus, if you expect too few others to contribute, you ought to contribute, because you'll make a 10% profit. Alternatively, if others contribute and you're nearing the threshold, you ought to contribute to ensure the threshold is met and the good is provided given that good's benefit to you exceeds the cost of your contribution (by hypothesis). Contributing is thus the *dominant strategy*: no matter what others do, you are better off contributing than not.

A closely related point concerns what are called common-pool resources. Common-pool resources are rivalrous but non-excludable. The resources are finite, so one person's consumption comes at the expense of others. But it is difficult or impossible to exclude people from using them. Examples include fish stocks in the ocean, or, arguably, the climate itself. (We "consume" good climate by polluting.) The ecologist Garrett Hardin argued that in such cases, people would have a strong incentive to overuse the resources and deplete them to nothing. He argued that the best mechanism to stop such "tragedies of the commons" is to empower a Leviathan to control everyone's behavior.

Nobel laureate Elinor Ostrom's empirical work shows that things are not so simple. She says, "What makes [Hardin's] models so dangerous—when they are used ... as the foundation for policy—is that the constraints that are assumed to be fixed for the purpose of analysis are taken on faith as being fixed in empirical settings ..."[9] In other words, Hardin thinks the Iron Fist of Omnipotent Government is necessary to solve problems because he didn't look around to see how real-life people solve such problems. Instead, what Ostrom finds is that when people face common-pool resource problems, they frequently resolve the problem without government intervention. Instead, they are able to create non-state accountability and enforcement structures which prevent people from overusing such resources.

Remember, all these points hold in the real world, where in fact many people are morally bad, where many people routinely violate principles 1–4. It's an interesting question to what degree we can maintain order without the state, even in a world full of rapacious, exploitative, predatory, imprudent, entitled, and nasty people, as we have in the real world. But here we're asking how well people would do if everyone were decent.

Decent agents *prefer* to contribute. They don't want to free ride. They will do their fair share "to promote just schemes" when they "believe that others, or sufficiently many of them, will do theirs."[10] Decent people want to overcome collective action problems and know others do too. They know that, say, an entrepreneur using a dominant assurance contract won't take the money and run, because that would be indecent.

Arguments for the state nearly always begin by imagining people acting badly and then imagining well-motivated governments rescuing us for such bad behavior.[11] But, if we want to argue that decent people need a state, we have to find grounds for a state even if no one ever does anything morally indecent.

THE ARISTOCRACY OF SELF-CONTROL?

Principle 3 requires us to act with basic prudence. Every twenty-year-old knows they will retire at some point. They can take steps right now to ensure that they have enough for retirement, such as saving and investing instead of buying luxuries. Investing $3000 a year in your twenties can more or less guarantee you'll retire a millionaire.

Some philosophers wonder whether asking people to exercise prudence is too demanding. Consider an old blog-post by Joseph Heath, where he wonders whether self-control is an aristocratic resource:

> Because I am self-conscious about my membership in the self-control aristocracy, I am acutely aware of the fact that, when I think about questions of "individual liberty" in society, I come to it with a particular set of class interests. That is because I stand to benefit much more from an expansion of the space of individual liberty than the average person does—because I have greater self-control. So I recognize that, while a 24-hour beer store would be great for me, it would be a mixed blessing for others. Or I recognize that my enthusiasm for the new TFSA program is not universally shared—not because its benefits flow primarily to the wealthy, but because its benefits flow primarily to the self-control aristocracy.

> What does this have to do with libertarianism? It is important because every academic proponent of libertarianism—understood loosely, as any doctrine that assigns individual liberty priority over other political values—is a member of the self-control aristocracy. As a result, they are advancing a political ideal that benefits themselves to a much greater extent than it benefits other people. In most cases, however, they do so naively, because they do not recognize themselves as members of an elite, socially-dominant group, that stands to benefit disproportionately. They think of liberty as something that creates an equal benefit for all. (Or, to the extent that it fails to benefit some people, it is entirely the fault of those people, for failing to exercise sufficient self-control.)[12]

To be fair to Heath, he means that the academic libertarians he knows tend to have unusually high levels of self-control. For them, prudence comes easily. So, he thinks, they imagine how society would go if only everyone had such high levels of self-control and prudence.

Recall that Cohen argues that citing sociological trends in human behavior is not enough to prove that people can't behave better. We can predict that businesspeople in high-stress environments will lie and cheat more than those in low-stress environments. We can predict that students will cheat more when they have one final exam worth 100% of their grades than if they have many smaller assignments. We can predict that a person who undergoes hazing rituals is more likely to haze others. And so on. None of these things eliminate moral agency; none of these things render people unable do better and thus not responsible for their actions.

Let's ask: does this apply even to poor adults in developed countries in the West? Are they responsible for any imprudent choices they make which lead to or reinforce their poverty? Note that I'm not asking about children born in poverty (they can't choose their parents) or people who live in undeveloped or poor countries. I'm asking about poor adults in rich countries. Note that I'm not asking whether people have complete control over their lives—of course, they don't—nor am I asking whether systematic injustice makes it harder for some to be rich than others—of course, it does.

The Brookings Institute, a moderately left-wing think tank, published a famous series of papers showing that poor American teenagers can almost guarantee they will enter and remain in the middle class if they follow three simple rules: "finish high school, get a full-time job and wait until age 21 to get married and have children."[13] These rules are causal, not mere correlations. In most cases, following them causes you to become middle class (by American standards, and thus rich by world standards); failure to follow them makes you become or remain poor. If an American teenager follows these three rules, she has only a 2% chance of being poor (by rich American standards) as an adult, and a 75% chance of ending up in the middle class, defined as her making at least $55,000 a year, which puts her in the top few percent of world income earners.

Is this too demanding? A massive literature in economics, sociology, and anthropology confirms that the Western poor often make self-destructive choices. For instance, low-income families are more likely to experience teen pregnancy.[14] People in low-income households are more likely to abuse cigarettes or illicit drugs.[15] They are more likely to engage in heavy drinking.[16] They are more likely to be obese and suffer the resulting health problems; careful empirical work by economics shows a significant part of this problem is caused by self-control issues rather than exogenous factors.[17] (This is one reason why attempts to provide cheap healthy food have failed; even when the poor can afford healthy foods, they disproportionately choose not to eat them.[18]) They are far more likely to commit crime.[19] The poor demonstrate lower levels of conscientiousness, for instance, as measured by the Stanford marshmallow experiment,[20] and higher rates of impulsivity.[21]

Note that neither the Brookings studies (and those like it) nor I deny that many poor people are worse off in part because they were dealt a bad hand, because their ancestors were mistreated, or because they face systematic biases or racism today. It's generally easier for upper middle-class kids than lower-class kids to become upper-middle class adults. None of this denies that it's harder or much harder for some people to succeed than others thanks to external factors beyond their control. Brookings isn't saying that a poor kid born in a blighted rural town has it as easy as the average student at Eton or Phillips Andover.

Cohen says that sociological factors do not excuse the rich and middle-class people he wishes to condemn as too selfish for socialism. The fact that you are socialized in a competitive business environment to pursue the bottom line doesn't excuse you when you exploit, defraud, or mistreat others in pursuit of profit. What would he say about poor people who are socialized around imprudent behaviors? (Of course, not all poor people are so socialized. But here I am asking about those who are.)

I know what he *should* say, but I don't know what he would say. What he should say is that even if people in poverty feel more social or peer pressure to act in self-destructive and imprudent ways, this does not suffice to prove they *cannot* act differently or even that they face exculpatory conditions. To excuse these behaviors, one must show that the poor lack the mental capacity to choose better or are under severe external duress. It's not enough to show that they have things *harder* than more privileged people. You have to show they *can't* do better than they do.

You might not agree with Cohen (and me) that people "can" do better. But if not, you face a kind of dilemma here. One option is to deny the poor have the agency to get a secondary school diploma or equivalent, hold any job for six months, or use condoms. The upside of that, if there is one, is that it avoids the discomfort of blaming people for imprudence. The downside is that it treats the western poor as subhuman, non-agents. The person who takes this view is stuck saying something like this: "In my view, the typical poor person in the United States is clinically incapable of using condoms, getting any job, and completing a high school diploma. Asking a poor person to use condoms is like asking a person with a severe, pathological phobia of the dark and of insects to spend an evening at the bottom of a well. Or, indeed, it is like asking a schizophrenic person to stop hallucinating."

Note that when I've presented papers on this issue, many polite left-wing professors responded that they in fact agree with that statement. I asked them if I could quote them or cite them, but they all asked me not to. I think we know why. You have to say something like that to avoid blaming the Western poor, but then you express contempt for their agency.

The other option is to say that the Western poor could make better choices, and that does not require superhuman levels of prudence. But this view has the cost of requiring us to think that most poor adults in developed countries are to a significant degree blameworthy for their poverty and their destructive choices. That's costly and uncomfortable, if not nearly as bad as the other option.

At any rate, remember that if people were *minimally decent*, many of the external factors harming the poor and making it more difficult to succeed would disappear. There would be no more racism, classism, exploitation, rights-deprivations, crime, and the like. In our real world, full of injustice, most people in the West remain moral agents who are responsible for the choices they make, and they could make themselves better off. In a world where everyone is decent, we may not realize the Mickey Mouse Clubhouse Village utopia, but we would remove most of the systematic barriers that make success hard.

ANARCHISM AS A RESEARCH QUESTION

In the real world, many people are indecent. They do not simply fall short of being angels. They seek to dominate, abuse, and oppress others. They lie, cheat, and steal. They don't think to the future and feel entitled to shift the resulting burdens and bad consequences onto innocent others. They want to free ride inside collective action problems. We live among people who kill bicyclists to make a cool TikTok, or who oppress hundreds of millions of people to keep themselves in power, or who lie to keep their jobs when they cause a pandemic.

In the real world, because many people are morally bad, we have to devise enforcement institutions and strategies to produce better behavior. These include things like reputation mechanisms (such as gossip, seller/buyer ratings, consumer review magazines, and the like) and violence. If everyone were merely decent, we would have no need to use violence to enforce our rights. In a world where no one murders, rapes, or steals, you don't need weapons to stop others from murdering, raping, or stealing.

Most people conclude that moral indecency creates the need for the state. After all, they reason, many people are bad, and so we need effective, safe, and organized protection from those bad people. But moral indecency also creates reasons to fear a state. After all, they should also reason, many people are bad, and every page of every history book and every current newspaper indicates that governments are filled with such morally indecent people.

Consider the four most common reasons people claim we need a state:

1. *Protection goods*: The state is necessary (or the best means) of providing protection for life, liberty, and property.
2. *Public goods*: The state is necessary (or the best means) of providing public goods, such as certain forms of roads.
3. *Social Insurance*: The state is necessary (or the best means) of providing insurance against misfortune.
4. *Regulation*: The state is necessary (or the best means) of preventing market failure.

Even in our world full of indecent people who fail to do the moral minimum, whether some form of anarchism could supply these things. I think whether various forms of anarchism can substitute for the state is an open research question. However, if people were just decent, we wouldn't need a state at all.

Cohen's socialist ideal is not, in my view, an ideal at all. But it is indeed very demanding, and we don't live up to its demands. Cooperative capitalist anarchism is an ideal, but it turns out not all that demanding. We fall short because we are indecent, not because we aren't angels.

ON SKEPTICISM ABOUT UTOPIAN THEORIZING

What kind of capitalism is best in the real world, given how flawed real people are? I haven't attempted to answer that question in this book; I leave that for my other books and articles.

Cohen, Estlund, and many other philosophers think that justice is what obtains in a society full of people who are fully committed to justice and always do what justice requires. They think we should never dumb down the requirements of justice to accommodate people's widespread and predictable moral failings. Instead, such failings are failings; they show people are unjust.

Some philosophers disagree. For instance, Gregory Kavka and Gerald Gaus claim that even perfectly moral people would have entrenched moral disagreements that would bring them into conflict with one another.[22] Kavka thinks this means even angels would need a state.[23] Gaus thinks it means the concept of utopia is incoherent.

I don't think they're right, but the good news for me and this book is that it doesn't matter if they are. Cohen and other socialists believe that they seize the moral high ground by insisting on a certain kind of ideal theory. They think that capitalists defend capitalism only by excusing morally depraved attitudes. Cohen more or less concedes that capitalism "wins" if we do political philosophy the way Gaus or other ideal theory skeptics think we should. But in this book, I've granted Cohen his way of doing philosophy, but then shown that it doesn't generate his socialist conclusions.

If skepticism about utopian theorizing is right, capitalism wins over socialism. If utopian theorizing is valid, capitalism also wins over socialism. Either way, we should endorse some form of capitalism over some form of socialism. So, the case for capitalism does not depend on esoteric questions about proper methods in philosophy.

Notes

Deep Down, Everyone's a Socialist ... and Wrong

1. Calculations according to the "How Rich Am I?" calculator at www.givingwhatwecan.org, and Milanovic 2007.
2. Schmidtz and Brennan 2010, 190.
3. Smith 1981, 26–27.
4. Mandeville 1988 24.
5. Mandeville 1988, 26.
6. Burns 2011.
7. Rand had an esoteric understanding of "selfishness" and a bizarre understanding of "altruism," but the point remains.
8. This was not always the case. Socialists used to argue that socialism would be more efficient than capitalism. They argued that socialism was going to make everyone rich. It was only when it became clear that socialism didn't work that they switched primarily to moral arguments.
9. Quoted in Pinker 2003, 296.
10. Poole 2009.
11. Wood 2009, 27.
12. Barker 2009.
13. Stone 2009.
14. Cohen 2009, 10.
15. Cohen 2009. 7.
16. Cohen 2009, 9.
17. Actually, Cohen seems to betray some misunderstanding here. Cohen keeps having his capitalist campers demand that they be *richer* than the others. He has them concerned not to improve their absolute, but their relative level of welfare. Maybe some people are like that. But

most people are more concerned with doing better, period, not doing better than the Jones.

18. Cohen 2009, 36.
19. Cohen 2009, 38.
20. Cohen 2008, 13.
21. Cohen 1995, 256.
22. Estlund 2008, 269–270.
23. The institutions of the USSR seemed to function much like this magic fog.
24. Gall 2013.
25. Gall 2013.
26. I'm pretty sure I got this idea from Pete Boettke.
27. Store managers can decide by fiat on the sticker price of a good by fiat, but they cannot usually decide by fiat what the good will actually sell for. If they set the price too high, people won't buy it, and if they set it too low, it will fly off the shelves and be resold at a higher price in the secondary market.
28. In the language of economics, in this scenario, there has been both a supply and a demand shock. There is a supply shock, because the lack of power makes it harder to produce ice or prevent the current stock from melting. There is a demand shock, because the power outage means that more people need ice and are willing to pay more for it.
29. Small-scale socialism—a 100-person commune—works, under some conditions, because everything interacts face-to-face. But a country like China, with a population of 1.34 billion, is not a commune.
30. E.g., Cohen 1983, 24.
31. See, e.g., Cohen 2000, 101–115.
32. Cohen 2009, 60. Cohen says very few "socialist economists [*sic*] would now dissent from [the] proposition" that "it becomes more difficult to know what to produce, and how to produce it, without the device of market signals."
33. Of course, Carens is not the first to propose market socialism as a solution to the Calculation Problem. In fact, most of the historical debate over the Calculation Problem concerned not whether central planning would work, but whether market socialism would avoid the problems of central planning. Instead, Carens is trying to revive a

debate about market socialism and make a better case for it than his intellectual predecessors did.

34. Cohen 2009, 82.
35. Cohen 2000, 118.
36. Cohen 2000, 118.
37. E.g., economist Deirdre McCloskey, in conversation.
38. Cohen 2009, 53.
39. Cohen 2009, 76.
40. Cohen 2009, 78.
41. Cohen 2009, 78.

The Mickey Mouse Clubhouse Argument for Capitalism: A Parody

1. Cohen 1995 is a critique of Nozick 1974. I think Cohen's critique is based on a misunderstanding, but that's a topic for another day.
2. N.B. in the real *Mickey Mouse Clubhouse* TV show, Mickey often takes the lead on certain collective projects, but everyone consents to this, because they acknowledge he has superior judgment when it comes to solving the funny problems the villagers encounter. Donald has a few small character flaws (for comedic effect). Pete sometimes plays a semi-antagonistic role, but usually only when he appears not as himself, but as a special variation of himself, such as "Plundering Pete" or "Space Pirate Pete," who is not a part of the village and is not supposed to be the real Pete. Even when Pete does play a minor villain, he always learns the error of his ways and by the end of the episode becomes fully virtuous. The purpose of these character flaws is to teach toddlers moral lessons. But all this is incidental to my argument here. We can just imagine a *Mickey Mouse Clubhouse* show in which Mickey had the same status as everyone else, Donald was less grumpy, and Pete less mischievous.
3. Cohen rejects the idea that our bodies belong to us. See Cohen 1995. See also the work of his student, Cecile Fabre (2006).
4. Cohen 1995
5. Lenin 1919, 497.
6. Amis 2002, 79.
7. Amis 2002, 69.

8. Amis 2002, 107.
9. Vladimir Lenin, quoted in Midlarsky 2011, 127.
10. This is what Soviet Premier Nikita Krushchev said during his visit to the US in 1959. See Schmidtz and Brennan 2010, 120.
11. Quoted from Occupy Wall Street 2011.
12. Rawls 1971, 3.
13. Rush, "Closer to the Heart," from *A Farewell to Kings*. Neil Peart, the lyricist and drummer, describes himself as a "bleeding heart libertarian" (Greene 2012).
14. Mankiw 2001, 12.
15. Volokh 2010.

Human Nature and Justice

1. Nozick 1974, 183.
2. All of this is how Cohen—and many other philosophers—interpret Rawls's argument. However, Arneson 2008 argues this interpretation is mistaken. I will not pursue this point here, because I want to argue that Cohen's argument fails even if we grant him his interpretation of Rawls.
3. See Cohen 2009; Miller 2012; Estlund 2014; Schmidtz 2014; Stemplowska and Swift 2012.
4. Cohen 2008; Cohen 2003. For a sustained critique of this way of theorizing, see Farelly 2007.
5. Singer 1972.
6. The comedian Louis C. K. jokes in a Singerian spirit, "My life is really evil. There are people who are starving in the world, and I drive an Infiniti. That's really evil … There are people who are like born and then they go, 'Oh, I'm hungry,' and then they just die, and that's all they ever got to do. And, meanwhile, I'm in my car—boom boom, brrr!—like having a great time, and I sleep like a baby … I could trade my Infiniti for like a really good car, like a nice Ford Focus … and I'd get back like twenty thousand dollars, and I could save hundreds of people from dying of starvation with that money. And every day, I don't do it." See www.youtube.com/watch?v=lC4FnfNKwUo.
7. Estlund 2019. The next few paragraphs borrow from Brennan 2022.
8. Estlund 2019, 102.
9. Estlund 2019, 102–103.

10. Estlund 2019, 103–104.
11. E.g., Scheffler 1992, 102–110.
12. Estlund 2019, 107–111.
13. Estlund 2019, 112.
14. See Caplan 2007.
15. In fact, Rawls later claimed his theory is only compatible with the watered-down capitalism of "property-owning democracy" and the market-socialism of "liberal socialism." But, as I explain later, this is in part because Rawls himself makes certain mistakes Cohen makes. Rawls also became increasingly uncomfortable with the nearly limitless inequality his theory seemed to justify, and so added in a series of what look like ad hoc modifications in order to generate greater equality. On this point, see Tomasi 2008 and Brennan 2007.
16. Schmidtz 2014.
17. Cf. Stemplowska and Swift 2012, 384.
18. Rawls 2001, 178.
19. Shapiro 2007, 6.
20. Buchanan 2003, 15.
21. E.g., Rawls 2001, 137: "Much conservative thought has focused on the last three questions mentioned above, criticizing the ineffectiveness of the welfare state and its tendencies toward waste and corruption. But here we focus largely on the first question, leaving the others aside. We ask: what kind of regime and basic structure would be right and just, could it be effectively and workably maintained?"
22. Rawls 2001, 136, says there are four basic questions we can ask about a regime:
    A. Are the regime's institutions right and just?
    B. Could a regime's institutions be effectively designed to realize its declared goals?
    C. Would citizens comply with the regime's institutions and with whatever rules apply to them?
    D. Would citizens be competent to play whatever role they hold?

    He tells us (Rawls 2001, 137) that we should put aside questions B-D and just focus on question A, asking what kind of regime would just if it could be workably maintained.

23. Krause 2010, 885.
24. The utopian socialist Charles Fourier predicted that under socialism we would transform the oceans into lemonade. He was a bit of a nut.
25. Zak 2008, xv.
26. Gintis 2012.
27. Zak and Knack, 2001.
28. Al-Ubayli et al. 2013. I discuss further studies in Brennan and Jaworski 2015.
29. E.g., Ostrom 2003; De Soto 2000; Richerson and Boyd 2008; McCloskey 2011; North 1990; Zak and Knack 2001.
30. For more on the role of trust, see Schmidtz and Brennan 2010.
31. Transparency International 2012.
32. See Brennan and Jaworski 2022 for a longer summary of this work.

Why Utopia Is Capitalist

1. Schmidtz and Brennan 2010, 36.
2. Hume 1975, 183–192.
3. Hume 1975, 184–185.
4. Schmidtz 2008, 193–210.
5. Gaus 2012, 96.
6. For a more developed rendition of this argument, see Lomasky 1987, 25–27, 119–124, passim.
7. Nozick 1990, 72–76.
8. Schmidtz and Brennan 2010, 133.
9. I take these ideas from Schmidtz 2006, 31, 166.
10. Cohen 1995, 58.
11. See, e.g., Krugman and Wells 2009, chapters 1, 2, 4, passim; Mankiw 2008, 8–12, Part III; Weil 2009, chapters 2, 10–12, 17; Ekelund, Ressler, and Tollison chapters 1–4, 12–13; Alston, Kearl, and Vaughan 1992; McConnell, Brue, and Flynn 2010, chapters 1–4, 7, 9, 11, passim; Schmidtz and Brennan 2010, chapters 2 and 4.
12. Tomasi 2012, 77.
13. Nozick 1974, 297–334.
14. Nozick 1974, 310.
15. Nozick 1974, 310.
16. For more on this, see Lomasky 2002.

17. For instance, Cohen 2000, 181, tells a story about how his father was fired from his job, and then says that the problem with capitalism is that it requires people to handle one another. He's right—in real-life capitalism, people do "handle" one another, and there's something repugnant about that. But in real-life socialism, people also handle one another in repugnant ways. In utopian socialism—the kind of socialism Cohen advocates—they don't, but neither do they in utopian capitalism.
18. Nozick (1999) argues that the available empirical evidence suggests that at most only about 6–9% of people would choose socialism. Nozick's argument is that we should look to Israel, where the kibbutzim are prosperous and well-respected, and where there is a long tradition of viewing socialism as the highest form of life. Even there, where there are few materialist or selfish reasons to choose capitalism over socialism, only 6–9% of people actually choose socialism.

Anti-Social Egalitarianism?

1. Gelonesi 2015.
2. D'Alessandro 2022.
3. See Brennan 2020.
4. Cohen 1995.
5. Fabre 2006.
6. Some philosophers (e.g., Barnes 2016) deny this.
7. Cohen 2009, 317.
8. Cohen 2009, 317–318.
9. Cohen 2009, 318.
10. See Cohen 2009.
11. Ackerman 1980, 31.
12. Ackerman 1983.
13. Dworkin 2001.
14. Weil 2013, 453.
15. Weil 2013, 450–451.
16. Cohen 2009, 17.
17. Cohen 2009, 37.
18. Cohen 2008, 2, says that "in a society in which distributive justice prevails, people's material prospects are roughly equal"; justice does not allow the "deep inequality" allowed by "John Rawls and his followers."

19. Cohen 2009, 24–25.
20. Cohen 2009, 30–31.
21. Cohen 2009, 31.
22. Cohen 2008, 181. Emphasis mine.
23. Cohen 2009, 35.
24. Otteson 2014, 73.
25. Cohen 2009, 35–36.
26. Cohen 2009, 38.
27. Otteson 2014, 73–74.
28. Lomasky 2002, 71–72.
29. Cohen 2008.

How Demanding Is Utopian Anarchism?

1. Madison 1788.
2. Brennan 2023.
3. Cohen 2009, 42.
4. Cohen 2009, 38–39.
5. This quotes Moller 2019, 3, except for the first sentence. Moller uses a case of someone who claims they have fallen onto hard times through no fault of their own. But I am considering the even easier case where someone didn't exercise basic prudence.
6. Stringham 2015, 5.
7. Hasnas 2008
8. Stringham 2015.
9. Ostrom 1990, 6.
10. Rawls 1971, 236.
11. See Brennan and Freiman 2022.
12. This quotation was retrieved from http://induecourse.ca/what-do-libertarians-and-pedophiles-have-in-common but is no longer accessible.
13. Haskins 2013.
14. Manlove et al. 2000a, 2000b; Sucoff and Upchurch 1988.
15. Baptiste-Roberts and Hossain 2018, 112.
16. Beaulier and Caplan 2007, 495.
17. Cutler, Glaeser, and Shapiro 2003.
18. An and Sturm 2012; Lee 2012.

19. Carlen 1988; Patterson 1991; Ludwig, Duncan, and Hirschfield 2001; Berk, Lenihan, and Rossi 1980; Nikulina, Widom, and Czaja, 2011; Ilan 2015.
20. Duncan and Hoffman 1991; Sutin, Evans, and Zonderman 2013; Letkiewicz and Fox 2014; Bogg and Roberts 2013.
21. Burdick, Roy, and Raver 2013; Lynam 2000; Murali and Oyebode 2010; Payne 2005.
22. Kavka 2005; Gaus 2016.
23. For a refutation, see Brennan and Freiman 2022.

Bibliography

Ackerman, Bruce. 1980. *Social Justice in the Liberal State*. New Haven: Yale University Press.

Ackerman, Bruce. 1983. "On Getting What We Don't Deserve," *Social Philosophy and Policy* 1: 60–70.

Alston, Richard M., J. R. Kearl, and Michael B. Vaughan. 1992. "Is There a Consensus Among Economists in the 1990's?,"*American Economic Review* 82: 203–209.

Al-Ubayli, Omar, Daniel Houser, John Nye, Maria Pia Paganelli, and Xiaofei Sophia Pan. 2013. "The Causal Effect of Market Priming on Trust: An Experimental Investigation Using Randomized Control," *PLoS One* 8(3): e55968. doi: 10.1371/journal.pone.0055968

Amis, Martin. 2002. *Koba the Dread: Laughter and the Twenty Million*. New York: Vintage, 2002.

An, Ruopeng, and Roland Sturm. 2012. "School and Residential Neighborhood Food Environment and Diet Among California Youth," *American Journal of Preventive Medicine* 42: 129–135.

Arneson, Richard. "Justice Is Not Equality," *Ratio* 21 (2008): 371–391.

Baptiste-Roberts, Kesha, and Mian Hossain. 2018. "Socioeconomic Disparities and Self-Reported Substance Abuse-Related Problems," *Addiction & Health* 10: 112.

Barker, Alexander. 2009. "On a Socialist Camping Trip," *The Oxonian Review* 10, www.oxonianreview.org/wp/you-and-i-and-a-whole-bunch-of-other-people-go-on-a-camping-trip

Barnes, Elizabeth. 2016. *The Minority Body*. Oxford: Oxford University Press.

Beaulier, Scott, and Bryan Caplan. 2007. "Behavioral Economics and Perverse Effects of the Welfare State," *Kyklos* 60: 485–507.

Berk, Richard, Kenneth Lenihan, and Peter H. Rossi. 1980. "Crime and Poverty: Some Experimental Evidence from Ex-Offenders," *American Sociological Review* 766–786.

Bogg, Tim, and Brent W. Roberts. 2013. "The Case for Conscientiousness: Evidence and Implications for a Personality Trait Marker of Health and Longevity," *Annals of Behavioral Medicine* 45: 278–288.

Brennan, Jason. 2007. "Rawls's Paradox," *Constitutional Political Economy* 18: 287–299.

Brennan, Jason. 2020. "Against the Moral Powers Test of Basic Liberty," *European Journal of Philosophy* 28: 492–505.

Brennan, Jason. 2022. "'Get a Job and Pay Your Taxes!': What Utopophiles Must Say to the Western Poor," *Social Philosophy and Policy* 39: 48–67.

Brennan, Jason and Christopher Freiman. 2022. "Why Not Anarchism?," *Politics, Philosophy, and Economics* 21: 415–436.

Brennan, Jason, and Peter Jaworski. 2015. *Markets without Limits*. New York: Routledge.

Buchanan, James. 2003. "Politics without Romance." *Policy* 19: 13–18.

Burdick, Jessica, Amanda Roy, and C. Cybele Raver. 2013. "Evaluating the Iowa Gambling Task as a Direct Assessment of Impulsivity with Low-Income Children," *Personality and Individual Differences* 55: 771–776.

Burns, Jennifer. 2011. *Goddess of the Market: Ayn Rand and the American Right*. New York: Oxford University Press.

Caplan, Bryan. 2007. *The Myth of the Rational Voter*. Princeton: Princeton University Press.

Carlen, Pat. 1988. *Women, Crime, and Poverty*. Milton Keynes: Open University Press.

Cohen, G. A. 1983. "The Structure of Proletariat Unfreedom," *Philosophy and Public Affairs* 12: 3–33.

Cohen, G. A. 1995. *Self-Ownership, Freedom, and Equality*. New York: Oxford University Press, 1995.

Cohen, G. A. 2000. *If You're an Egalitarian, How Come You're So Rich?* Cambridge, MA: Harvard University Press.

Cohen, G. A. 2003. "Facts and Principles," *Philosophy and Public Affairs* 31: 211–245.

Cohen, G. A. 2008. *Rescuing Justice and Equality*. Cambridge, MA: Harvard University Press.

Cohen, G. A. 2009. *Why Not Socialism?* Princeton: Princeton University Press.

Cutler, David, Glaeser, Edward, and Shapiro, Jesse M.. 2003. "Why Have Americans Become More Obese?" *Journal of Economic Perspectives* 17: 93–118.

D'Alessandro, William. 2022. "Is It Bad to Prefer Attractive Partners?," *Journal of the American Philosophical Association*, online first edition, www.cambridge.org/core/journals/journal-of-the-american-philosophical-association/article/is-it-bad-to-prefer-attractive-partners/474E8BE49F985EB897B05255159689EE

De Soto, Hernando. 2000. *The Mystery of Capital*. New York: Basic Books.

Duncan, Greg J., and Saul D. Hoffman. 1991. "Teenage Underclass Behavior and Subsequent Poverty: Have the Rules Changed," in Christopher Jencks and Paul E. Peterson (eds.), *The Urban Underclass*, 155–174. Washington, DC: Brookings Institution Press.

Dworkin, Ronald. 2001. *Sovereign Virtue*. Cambridge, MA: Harvard University Press.

Ekelund, Robert, Rand Ressler, and Robert Tollison. 2006. *Microeconomics: Private and Public Choice*. New York: Prentice Hall.

Encyclopaedia Britannica. 1964. "Capitalism." In *Encyclopaedia Britannica*, volume 4, 840–844. Chicago: Encyclopaedia Britannica.

Estlund, David. 2008. *Democratic Authority*. Princeton: Princeton University Press.

Estlund, David. 2019. *Utopophobia*. Princeton: Princeton University Press.

Fabre, Cecile. 2006. *Whose Body Is It Anyway?* New York: Oxford University Press.

Farelly, Colin. 2007. "Justice in Ideal Theory: A Refutation." *Political Studies* 55: 844–864.

Gall, Jared. 2013. "Chevrolet Camaro ZL1 Convertible vs. 2012 BMW M6 Convertible," www.caranddriver.com/comparisons/2012-bmw-m6-convertible-page-2

Gaus, Gerald. 2012. "Property," in David Estlund (ed.), *The Oxford Handbook of Political Philosophy*. New York: Oxford University Press.

Gaus, Gerald. 2016. "The Commonwealth of Bees: On the Impossibility of Justice-through-Ethos," *Social Philosophy and Policy* 33: 96–121.

Gelonesi, Joe. 2015. "Is Having a Loving Family an Unfair Advantage?" www.abc.net.au/listen/programs/philosopherszone/new-family-values/6437058

Gintis, Herbert. 2012. "Giving Economists Their Due," *Boston Review*, June 25, www.bostonreview.net/gintis-giving-economists-their-due

Greene, Andy. 2012. "Neil Peart on Rush's New LP and Being a 'Bleeding Heart Libertarian'," www.rollingstone.com/music/news/q-a-neil-peart-on-rushs-new-lp-and-being-a-bleeding-heart-libertarian-20120612

Haskins, Ron. 2013. "Three Simple Rules Poor Teens Should Follow to Join the Middle Class," www.brookings.edu/opinions/three-simple-rules-poor-teens-should-follow-to-join-the-middle-class/

Hasnas, John. 2008. "The Obviousness of Anarchy." In R. Long and T. Machan (eds.), *Anarchism/Minarchism: Is Government Part of a Free Country*. Farnham: Ashgate Press.

Hume, David. 1975. *Enquiries Concerning Human Understanding and Concerning the Principles of Morals*, ed. L. A. Selby-Bigge and P. H. Nidditich, 3rd edition. New York: Oxford University Press.

Ilan, Jonathan. 2015. *Understanding Street Culture: Poverty, Crime, Youth and Cool*. New York: Macmillan International Higher Education.

Krause, Sharon. 2010. "Beyond Capitalism?" *Political Theory* 38: 884–890.

Krugman, Paul, and Robin Wells. 2009. *Economics*, 2nd edition. New York: Worth Publishers.

Lee, Helen. 2012. "The Role of Local Food Availability in Explaining Obesity Risk Among Young School-Aged Children," *Social Science and Medicine* 74: 1193–1203.

Lenin, V. I. 1919. "Letter from Lenin to Gorky, Sep. 15, 1919," in Library of Congress Revelations from the Russian Archives, www.loc.gov/exhibits/archives/g2aleks.html

Letkiewicz, Jodi C., and Jonathan J. Fox. 2014. "Conscientiousness, Financial Literacy, and Asset Accumulation of Young Adults," *Journal of Consumer Affairs* 48: 274–300.

Lomasky, Loren. 1987. *Persons, Rights, and the Moral Community*. New York: Oxford University Press.

Lomasky, Loren. 2002. "Nozick's Libertarian Utopia," in David Schmidtz (ed.), *Robert Nozick*, 59–82. New York: Cambridge University Press.

Ludwig, Jen, Duncan, Greg J., and Paul Hirschfield. 2001. "Urban Poverty and Juvenile Crime: Evidence from a Randomized Housing-Mobility Experiment," *The Quarterly Journal of Economics* 116: 655–679.

Lynam, Donald R. 2000. "The Interaction Between Impulsivity and Neighborhood Context on Offending: The Effects of Impulsivity Are Stronger in Poorer Neighborhoods," *Journal of Abnormal Psychology* 109: 563–574.

Madison, James. 1788. "Federalist Papers: Primary Documents in American History: Federalist Nos. 51–60," https://guides.loc.gov/federalist-papers/text-51-60

Mandeville, Bernard. 1988. *The Fable of the Bees*. Indianapolis: Liberty Fund.

Mankiw, N. Gregory. *Principles of Economics*, 5th edition. New York: Southwestern College Publishers.

Mankiw, N. Gregory. 2011. *Principles of Economics*, 6th edition. New York: Cengage Learning.

Manlove, Jennifer, Carrie Mariner, and Angela Romano Papillo. 2000a. "Subsequent Fertility Among Teen Mothers: Longitudinal Analyses of Recent National Data," *Journal of Marriage and Family* 62: 430–448.

Manlove, Jennifer, Elizabeth Terry, Laura Gitelson, Angela Romano Papillo, and Stephen Russell. 2000b. "Explaining Demographic Trends in Teenage Fertility, 1980–1995," *Family Planning Perspectives* 32: 166–175.

McCloskey, Deirdre. 2011. *Bourgeois Dignity*. Chicago: University of Chicago Press.

McConnell, Campbell, Stanley Brue, and Sean Flynn. 2010. *Economics*, 18th edition. New York: McGraw-Hill.

Midlarsky, Manus. 2011. *Origins of Political Extremism*. New York: Cambridge University Press.

Milanovic, Branko. 2007. *Worlds Apart: Measuring International and Global Inequality*. Princeton: Princeton University Press.

Miller, David. 2012. *Justice for Earthlings*. New York: Oxford University Press.

Moller, Dan. 2019. *Governing Least: A New England Libertarianism*. New York: Oxford University Press.

Murali, Vijaya, and Femi Oyebode. 2004. "Poverty, Social Inequality and Mental Health," *Advances in Psychiatric Treatment* 10: 216–224

Nikulina, Valentina, Cathy Spatz Widom, and Sally Czaja. 2011. "The Role of Childhood Neglect and Childhood Poverty in Predicting Mental Health, Academic Achievement and Crime in Adulthood," *American Journal of Community Psychology* 48: 309–321.

North, Douglas. 1990. *Institutions, Institutional Change, and Economic Performance*. New York: Cambridge University Press.

Nozick, Robert. 1974. *Anarchy, State, and Utopia*. New York: Basic Books.

Nozick, Robert. 1990. *The Examined Life*. New York: Simon and Schuster.

Nozick, Robert. 1999. *Socratic Puzzles*. Cambridge, MA: Harvard University Press.

Occupy Wall Street. 2011. "A Modest Call to Action on this September 17th," http://occupywallst.org/article/September_Revolution/

Ostrom, Elinor. 1990. *Governing the Commons*. Cambridge: Cambridge University Press.

Ostrom, Elinor (ed.). 2003. *Trust and Reciprocity: Interdisciplinary Lessons from Experimental Research*. New York: Russell Sage.

Patterson, E. Britt. 1991. "Poverty, Income Inequality, and Community Crime Rates," *Criminology* 29: 755–776.

Payne, Ruby. 2005. *A Framework for Understanding Poverty*. New York: Aha Process.

Pinker, Stephen. 2003. *The Blank Slate: The Modern Denial of Human Nature*. New York: Penguin.

Poole, Stephen. 2009. "Et Cetera: Why Not Socialism?," *The Guardian*, October 30, 2009, www.guardian.co.uk/books/2009/oct/31/nonfiction-book-roundup-steven-poole

Rawls, John. 1971. *A Theory of Justice*. Cambridge, MA: Harvard University Press.

Rawls, John. 2001. *Justice as Fairness: A Restatement*. Cambridge, MA: Harvard University Press.

Richerson, Peter J., and Robert Boyd. 2008. "The Evolution of Free Enterprise Values," in Paul Zak (ed.), *Moral Markets*, 107–141. Princeton: Princeton University Press.

Scheffler, Samuel. 1992. *Human Morality*. New York: Oxford University Press.

Schmidtz, David. 2006. *Elements of Justice*. New York: Cambridge University Press.

Schmidtz, David. 2008. *Person, Polis, Planet*. New York: Oxford University Press.

Schmidtz, David. 2014. "Idealism as Solipsism," in Serena Olsaretti (ed.), *Oxford Handbook of Distributive Justice*. New York: Oxford University Press.

Schmidtz, David, and Jason Brennan. 2010. *A Brief History of Liberty*. Oxford: Wiley-Blackwell.

Shapiro, Daniel. 2007. *Is the Welfare State Justified?* New York: Cambridge University Press.

Singer, Peter. 1972. "Famine, Affluence, and Morality," *Philosophy and Public Affairs* 1: 229–243.

Smith, Adam. 1981. *An Inquiry into the Nature and Causes of the Wealth of Nations, Vol I*. Indianapolis: Liberty Fund.

Stemplowska, Zofia, and Adam Swift. 2012. "Ideal and Non-Ideal Theory," in David Estlund (ed.), *The Oxford Handbook of Political Philosophy*. New York: Oxford University Press.

Stringham, P. Edward. 2015 *Private Governance: Creating Order in Economic and Social Life*. New York: Oxford University Press.

Stone, Andrew. 2009. "Why Not Socialism?," *Socialist Review*, November, www.socialistreview.org.uk/article.php?articlenumber=11028

Sucoff, Clea A., and Dawn M. Upchurch. 1998. "Neighborhood Context and the Risk of Childbearing Among Metropolitan-Area Black Adolescents," *American Sociological Review* 571–585.

Sutin, Angelina, Michele Evans, and Alan B. Zonderman. 2013. "Personality Traits and Illicit Substances: The Moderating Role of Poverty," *Drug and Alcohol Dependence* 131: 247–251.

Tomasi, John. 2008. *Free Market Fairness*. Princeton: Princeton University Press.

Transparency International. 2012. "Corruption Perceptions Index 2012," http://cpi.transparency.org/cpi2012/results

Volokh, Eugene. 2010. "Government Is Not Reason, It Is Not Eloquence—It Is Force," www.volokh.com/2010/04/14/government-is-not-reason-it-is-not-eloquence-it-is-force.

Weil, David. 2009. *Economic Growth*, 2nd edition. New York: Prentice Hall.

Wood, Ellen Meiksins. 2009. "Happy Campers," *London Review of Books* 32: 26–27.

Zak, Paul (ed.). 2008. *Moral Markets*. Princeton: Princeton University Press.

Zak, Paul, and Stephen Knack. 2001. "Trust and Growth," *Economic Journal* 111: 295–321.

Index

Note: Page numbers in bold indicate overarching discussions.

For Product Safety Concerns and Information please contact our EU representative GPSR@taylorandfrancis.com Taylor & Francis Verlag GmbH, Kaufingerstraße 24, 80331 München, Germany

Batch number: 10725833

Printed by Printforce, the Netherlands